HAUNTED HIGHWAY

THE SPIRITS OF ROUTE 66

ROUTE
US
66

by

Ellen Robson & Dianne Halicki

GOLDEN
WEST ☼
PUBLISHERS

Front cover art by Hugh Marshall

DEDICATION

This book is dedicated to our mothers, Lottie Halicki and Catherine Stroub, whose spirits took this trip with us.

Library of Congress Cataloging-in-Publication Data

Robson, Ellen
    Haunted Highway: the Spirits of Route US 66
       p.   cm.
    Includes bibliographical references and index.
    1. Haunted places — United States Highway 66. 2. Ghosts
    — United States Highway 66. 3. Ghost stories, American.
    4. United States Highway 66 — Miscellanea. I. Halicki,
    Dianne. II. Title.
    BF1472.U6R65   1999   99-24786
    133.1'0973—dc21   CIP

Printed in the United States of America

5th Printing © 2003

ISBN #1-885590-43-1

Golden West Publishers, Inc.
4113 N. Longview Ave.
Phoenix, AZ 85014, USA
(602) 265-4392
Visit our website: goldenwestpublishers.com

Table of Contents

Illinois

Missouri

Kansas, Oklahoma, Texas

New Mexico

New Mexico (Continued)

Arizona

Southern California

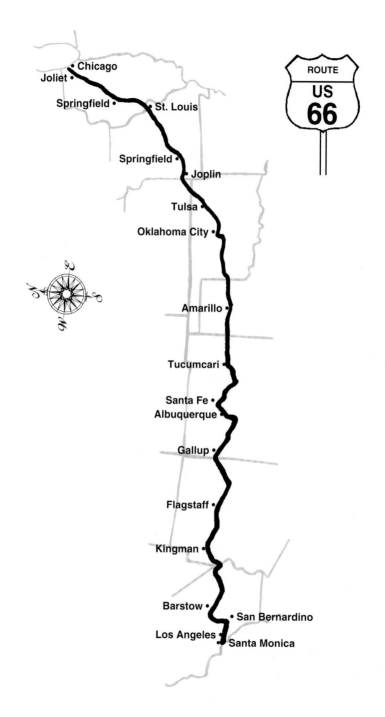

INTRODUCTION

It is no accident that Route 66 begins in Chicago–at Jackson Boulevard and Michigan Avenue. This route began long before anyone ever thought of the "Mother Road." It was started by adventurous souls who had already traveled this far west and began forging the haphazard trail even farther. They were seeking adventure, fame and fortune, or just a better life. They followed market routes, stagecoach routes and sometimes paths or trails that, patched together, made one continuous route. Paving the road made it easier for the rest of us to follow, but they were the first. Many of their spirits are still there, waiting for your visit.

This book begins in Chicago and follows Route 66, although our route is more like the pre-pavement days. You have to veer from the road here, jog there, but then Route 66 is all about travel and travel is about adventure and discovery. On this trip we discovered another world without ever straying far from America's main street. We got off to a phenomenal start in Chicago–no pun intended. Just pick a spot on a map of this city and you're likely to find a ghost nearby and someone ready to tell all about it. One could spend days ghost-hunting in Chicago, but we narrowed our selections to the most reliable sources and most interesting stories.

As we travel west, we'll take you off the route from time to time. We just couldn't take you so close to a good ghost story without stopping to hear it. Places like St. Charles, Missouri, Gutherie, Oklahoma, and Jerome, Arizona, were just too wonderful to pass by. We think you'll find the ghosts there well worth the side trip.

Keep in mind that we cannot guarantee a sighting. We did our best to conjure up some spirits when we took the trip. We climbed to a dark, dingy attic where the windows were so thick with dust that there was no evidence of any light outside. We picked our way down a path through a thick forest to find an old cemetery where the ghost of a woman carrying her baby had been seen. For all our effort, neither of us saw a ghost at either site.

We did experience the playful nature of one spirit, however. At LaPosada the resident ghost would not let us into her room until we brought up the concierge, who assured us that the ghost had nothing against us, she just likes to have fun.

That was our only encounter, but that doesn't mean that you won't see silverware float through the air while you're enjoying breakfast at the Birch Tree Inn. And you might just be awakened in the morning by the ghost of a little girl at the Stone Lion Inn.

Where ever we went we learned about the people who traveled this route long before us. Some led fascinating lives, some tragic, and some remain anonymous. For various reasons they have chosen to linger in our world after death.

Why they chose to stay was a big question for us. Once we acknowledged that these spirits really exist, we had to know why. So, we checked with the experts. When we asked David Oester, president of the International Ghost Hunters' Society, he came up with the most complete answer and we learned that there are different types of what we all refer to as ghosts.

The first type of spirit activity is called an intelligent haunting and is the most common. In this case, a spirit has stayed behind due to some type of unfinished business—waiting for a loved one or a need to take care of some injustice to themselves or a loved one. This group also includes those whose lives ended abruptly. Some are simply not done living, afraid to let go, or are confused and don't know how to cross over. These spirits may return to a place where they experienced happiness.

Sounds crazy? Let's say you're John Dillinger and you've just been shot down in the prime of your life. Who killed you? A man you've been thumbing your nose at for years. A man you were sure you could elude forever. If you were John Dillinger this might just seem like a bad dream to you, something that simply couldn't have happened. That might be why John Dillinger's ghost keeps running through the alley where he was shot, as if he were still trying to escape death.

A residual haunting is like a recording from the past. It can be something you see, like an apparition, or hear. In these cases it is as if the building itself has somehow captured a snippet from the past and continues to replay it sporadically– over and over. At Nat Antiques in Amarillo, Texas, visitors can hear the laughter of children who swam there long ago when it was a pool. That does not mean all those children are ghosts. This could well be a residual haunting.

There is one final explanation needed to cover all the situations we will present to you in this book. It may be the hardest to believe, but it does make sense, at least when you consider haunted cemeteries. This type of haunting is called a portal haunting. The portal is considered to be an opening from one world to the next that a spirit could travel through.

There are other types of hauntings but these three provide explanations for the situations we will be presenting. You may believe them, you may consider them to be bunk. But we couldn't take you on this trip without giving you some theories for why these ghosts exist.

One more thing you should know about ghosts is that evil spirits are few and far between. Spirits are simply disembodied entities. They have intelligence, emotions, and the same personalities they had as living beings. How many truly evil people do you know?

All of these sites are open to the public, so don't be afraid to go out and find them. You may have to buy a ticket, schedule a tour, or make a reservation, but in some you can simply walk in and have a cup of coffee. We tried to make it easier for you to do your own ghost hunting by giving you directions and phone numbers, and we urge you to call beforehand. Over the years, hours may change, or establishments may close. In any event, we hope you will pack your bags, grab this book and hit the road. If you prefer to be an armchair traveler, we still think you'll have an exciting trip along our haunted version of Route 66.

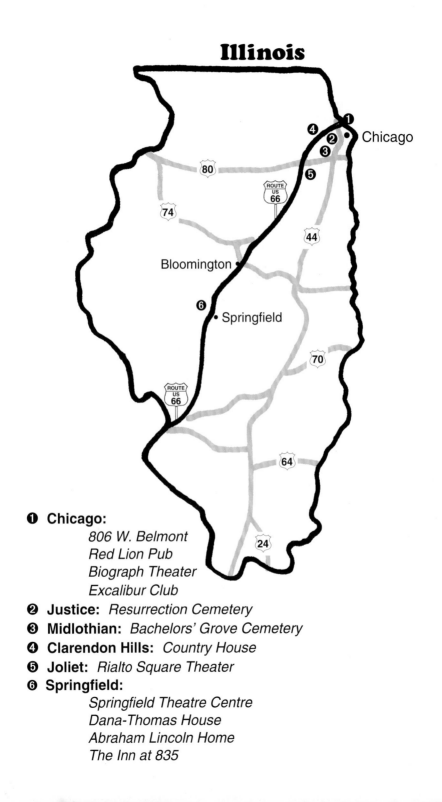

Illinois

Chicago

Bloomington

Springfield

❶ Chicago:
806 W. Belmont
Red Lion Pub
Biograph Theater
Excalibur Club

❷ Justice: *Resurrection Cemetery*

❸ Midlothian: *Bachelors' Grove Cemetery*

❹ Clarendon Hills: *Country House*

❺ Joliet: *Rialto Square Theater*

❻ Springfield:
Springfield Theatre Centre
Dana-Thomas House
Abraham Lincoln Home
The Inn at 835

806 WEST BELMONT

This building in the north end of downtown Chicago was originally built in 1879 as a private residence. Now in the middle of a busy shopping district, it has housed countless retail shops. Merchants are attracted by the retail site and frightened away by the ghosts.

When we visited 806 West Belmont it housed two businesses: Gosa-lo, a clothing store owned by Robert Pizarro, on the first floor, and House of Futons, owned by Samra Dupanovic, on the second. The third floor–the attic–houses the ghosts. Samra, who had recently moved her business into the building, had heard about the ghosts. Knowing she'd be using the attic for storage, she asked the owners what she might expect. Did people see the ghost? Did an apparition appear, or did they just feel something? They assured her they had never seen a ghost, they just had a feeling from time to time of someone standing behind them. When they turned, no one would be there.

Samra didn't have a problem with that. It sounded pretty mild for a ghost. In fact, she's still waiting for even that experience. Even though she's had no contact with the ghost, she's more than willing to share the reports she's heard from other people. One of her friends stopped by for a visit shortly after she opened for business. She wanted to explore the attic and Samra sent her up without any cautions. The woman returned immediately, saying she couldn't stay up there. She felt negative energy when she entered the attic and something told her to get out–fast! Samra told her friend the story about the ghost and the woman is sure that's what she encountered.

Stairway leading up to the attic at 806 West Belmont

Robert had just barely opened Gosa-lo before things started happening to him. While moving in, he hauled some boxes up to the attic. On his return, he saw that the boxes had been moved to the opposite end of the attic. No one else had moved them; the attic had been locked and no one else in the store had the key. On another occasion, he put out some candles that had been burning as he got ready to leave for the day. Before he left, something made him turn back. Robert could do little more than stare in amazement. He knew he'd put them out as the store was still full of the scent of extinguished candles. Yet there the candles were, burning brightly!

There have been reports of a woman walking to the stairs and vanishing, a cold spot in the attic and doors that open and close by themselves. There is also a report of a woman who was murdered in the basement in the 1880s, but Robert's aunt, a spiritualist, believes there are four ghosts. Coincidentally, four servants died in the attic when fire struck the house back when the original family owned it.

Both House of Futons and Gosa-lo have moved their shops to other locations: Robert says it is just too strange there. Victorian House Antiques, another former resident, has moved just a block up the street. 806 W. Belmont is prime real estate and will continue to attract merchants, just as it will probably continue to frighten them away.

Address: **806 West Belmont**
Chicago, IL 60657

Directions: Take I-55 east to Lake Shore Drive and head south for about 2 1/2 miles. Turn right on West Belmont.

RED LION PUB

When John Cordwell opened this English Pub in Chicago, he decided it would be a good opportunity to do something in memory of his father. The senior John Cordwell never had a headstone on his grave back in their homeland of England. John had installed a stained glass window over the landing, halfway up to the second floor of the pub. Beneath it he placed a brass plaque honoring his father. He felt that the elder Cordwell would be pleased with the gesture. The numerous spirits of the Red Lion Pub took it as an invitation to come out and play. They've been out ever since.

John has had many experiences with the spirits. He's felt taps on his shoulder and heard someone speaking to him as clearly as any human voice. When he's turned, no one is ever there. If he's imagining things, then so are plenty of his customers and employees who have experienced the same things.

Not long after John bought the building in 1984, he had the second floor converted from living space to restaurant space. On slow days the upstairs would be closed, yet people on the first floor could hear footsteps overhead. Employees would go up to find out who was there, but no one ever was.

One evening near closing time, the bartender closed the upstairs and came back down. Two police officers had stopped in for coffee and another bartender was working. No one else was in the building. All four jumped when they heard a crash upstairs that sounded as if a window had been broken. The officers unholstered their guns and proceeded upstairs. What

Second floor of the Red Lion Pub

they found was one barstool upside down. Everything else was in perfect order and no one was around.

The women's restroom upstairs seems to have a great deal of ghostly activity. There have been reports of screaming coming from inside. One evening an off-duty police officer was in the bar and heard the screaming. He tried to open to the door, but even though it had no lock, it wouldn't budge. The officer finally kicked the door in, only to find the bathroom empty. There are also reports of women stuck in the bathroom. One waitress worked on the door for 15 minutes, unable to get out, when suddenly the door opened by itself.

John Cordwell's father may be one of the ghosts who make the Red Lion Pub their home, but others have been around a long time. The previous owner used to invite other business owners in the area to come over and meet his invisible friends. A carpenter who lived on the second floor fifteen or twenty years earlier tried renovating the place. He would lock his tools behind the upstairs door whenever he left, but when he came back the padlocks were opened and the day's work was undone. Nails were pulled from boards and dropped on the floor. No one was ever around.

The building dates from 1882 and has had quite a checkered past. The ghosts may come from any one of the buildings incarnations–a bookie joint, a western saloon, apartments or a day care facility. Whoever they are, they don't seem to mean any harm and they sure make for an interesting evening.

Address:	**Red Lion Pub**
	2446 N. Lincoln Ave.
	Chicago, IL 60614
Phone:	(773) 348-2695
Hours:	12:00 pm to 1:00 am Daily

Directions: Take I-94 to Fullerton. Exit and head east on Fullerton to Lincoln. Turn west on Lincoln and go 1 1/2 miles to Red Lion Pub.

BIOGRAPH THEATER

On the night of July 22, 1934, John Dillinger, Public Enemy Number One, was leaving the Biograph Theater and walking right into the arms of death. Police and FBI agents were outside, waiting to ambush him. They did wait, in fact, until Dillinger had walked two doors down Lincoln Avenue and turned to enter a narrow alley, a short cut to Halstead Street. It wasn't until Dillinger reached for a concealed gun that police opened fire. Three shots hit and killed him.

Why had the police hesitated? What had given Dillinger the confidence to appear in public?

The answers may be the plastic surgery he'd had nearly two months earlier. His moles and scar were removed, his chin and nose altered, leaving several of the police and agents wondering just who this man was.

Another possibility involves one of his female companions. Dillinger had been seen entering the theater with two women, one in a red dress. This woman was said to have tipped off the feds that Dillinger would be at the theater for the performance of "Manhattan Melodrama." It was rumored that Dillinger, unable to get his hands on his stolen loot, was running low on cash. Perhaps this made the reward money, offered for Dillinger's arrest, look pretty good to his current sweetheart. Her need for ready cash might have made her convince the outlaw that he was ready for a public appearance.

Whatever fueled Dillinger's confidence, he underestimated his pursuers. Eventually they did recognize him and ended his career as a notorious gangster.

Biograph Theater

Surprisingly, it wasn't until the 1970s that reports of Dillinger's ghost began. The sightings were of a figure running down the alley, falling to the ground, and vanishing. Others reported cold spots in the alley.

Dillinger was so determined to survive that he'd had his features altered to elude the law in a day when plastic surgery was not a common practice. His spirit may still be clinging to life, refusing to cross over. Another theory is that since his death was sudden and traumatic, his spirit may not have had a chance to move on and still haunts the alley, lost and confused.

If you visit the Biograph, you can read the story of Dillinger's death and examine a diagram that details the FBI's setup and the last few minutes of John Dillinger's life. Both are posted in the window of the outside box office. Then walk south down the street and enter the alley—and decide for yourself if Public Enemy Number One is really dead.

Address: **Biograph Theater**
2433 N. Lincoln Ave.
Chicago, IL 60614

Phone: (773) 348-4123

Directions: Take I-94 to Fullerton. Exit and head east on Fullerton to Lincoln. Turn west on Lincoln and go 1 1/2 miles to the Biograph.

EXCALIBUR CLUB

The Excalibur nightclub in downtown Chicago, has a dark and tragic past, which explains a great deal about its haunted present. Two of Chicago's biggest disasters involve this popular club. At the time of the great fire of 1871, this building housed the Chicago Historical Society. The fire devastated much of Chicago and hit this building as well. As some historical society members were exiting the building, they believe some women may have run into the building to escape the fire. If they are right, the women may have perished inside.

A new building was erected on the same site, and the Historical Society moved back in. In 1915, a pleasure boat, the Eastland, was loaded with Western Electric employees and their families as part of an excursion across the lake for a picnic. A sudden rush of people toward one side of the boat caused it to capsize near the Clark Street Bridge, taking the lives of nearly 900 people. The owners of the Excalibur believe this was one of the buildings used as a temporary morgue.

Both tragedies left spirits and a spiritual energy behind that draws a clientele who are devotees of the occult and spiritualism. Many say they can feel the spiritual energy, not surprising since there are three known spirits in the Excalibur. A woman in her forties wearing a red dress was seen in a window and showed up in a Polaroid picture. An elderly man with a beard and a white tuxedo has appeared behind the bar. The spirit of a little girl rounds out the trio. Her spirit is believed to have come from the Eastland disaster along with the male spirit. They aren't certain of the woman's origins; she may

The Excalibur Club

be one of the women from the fire.

Wherever they come from, the employees can vouch for their activity. Scott Ward, the general manager, has watched many skeptical employees become believers after one or two encounters. One employee had been restocking the bars and was going in and out of a third floor storage room. As he walked through the door, he was stopped short by the sight of perfectly aligned rows of beer cases stacked up to the 22-foot ceiling. He'd been in the room just ten to twenty minutes before and the cases were piled as usual. It would have taken much more than twenty minutes and the help of a ladder for any person to have rearranged them in this manner. The employee called Scott in for an explanation but didn't want to hear anything about ghosts. Unfortunately, Scott had seen this type of thing before and that was the only explanation he could offer.

Scott is the type of person who needs to see such an event himself before he's willing to believe and he has seen plenty! One day he came in to find a 400–500 pound concrete statue sitting atop a stack of chairs. It takes three people to lug the statue from one spot to another when they clean the floors. It would have taken a lift to set it on top of the chairs. He has also closed down the building for the night, extinguishing 30 to 40 table candles before leaving. Upon his return one or two minutes later, the candles would be glowing again. This has happened not once, but many times.

The Dome Room seems to have most of the spiritual activity in the building. The domed ceiling is about 30 feet tall with a rim around the top. One day an employee walked in and saw a teddy bear balanced on the edge of the rim at least 25 feet up. Had it been tossed up there, it would have fallen into the curve of the rim. Someone would have needed a lift or scaffolding to reach the rim and balance the bear up there. Neither was available. It was eerie enough to see it up there, but the man left the room to get someone else to take a look. When he returned, the bear was sitting on the bar. The employees assume the little girl's spirit had a hand in this incident. She is also believed responsible for the table candles relighting, perhaps in fear of the dark.

People have also heard howling and crying from the bathroom downstairs, lights turn on and off by themselves, and the spiritual energy wreaks havoc on the alarm system due to the motion detectors in the dome room. All the employees were a little nervous when they first noticed the strange goings on there, and some still won't walk through the dome room alone. Others grew accustomed to the spirits and take their activities as just another part of their day.

Address:	Excalibur Club
	632 N. Dearborn
	Chicago, IL 60610
Phone:	(312) 266-1944
Hours:	5 pm - 4 am

Directions: From Michigan Avenue, turn right (east) onto East. Ontario Street. Go to Dearborn Street and turn right.

RESURRECTION CEMETERY

— — — — — — — — — — — — —

Motorists driving on Archer Street in Justice, a suburb of Chicago, are sometimes given a chance to pick up a phantom female hitchhiker. Resurrection Mary seems especially fond of young single men and has hopped into their cars uninvited, saying she needs a ride home. She has also been known to jump on the hoods of passing vehicles, regardless of whether the driver chooses to stop.

Mary, a young Polish girl, was killed in an automobile accident in 1934 on her way home after spending an evening dancing at the former O. Henry Ballroom, known now as the Willowbrook Ballroom. Only her first name is known, and because she is entombed at Resurrection Cemetery, the locals refer to her as Resurrection Mary. She was so fond of dancing that she was buried in her white ball-gown and black patent leather dancing shoes. She sometimes thumbs a ride to the Willowbrook Ballroom where she spends several hours dancing. Her dance partners always describe Mary as being very distant with icy cold skin. When she is ready to leave she simply asks a male to give her a ride home. Telling the driver to go north on Archer Street, she either disappears into thin air when they approach Resurrection Cemetery or she goes through the passenger car door and then floats through the cemetery gates.

In December of 1977, the police were called to Resurrection Cemetery with a report that a young girl, dressed in white, was grasping the iron bars, apparently locked in. By the time they

Resurrection Cemetery

arrived, the girl had vanished. When an officer tried to locate her with his spotlight, he discovered that the iron bars had been spread wide open with small handprints seared into the metal. Do the imprints belong to Mary?

Brian Stroub relates a story he'd heard about a sighting of Resurrection Mary. A friend's mother and aunt were driving past the cemetery gate when they observed a young girl with blonde hair. "They told me she was wearing a white dress and had a very pale complexion. She seemed to have a very luminous, florescent glow about her. After driving a few blocks they decided to turn around and take another look at her. She was still in front of the gate opening. She seemed to be walking but not making any distance."

This notorious hitchhiker has had a song written about her, "The Ballad of Resurrection Mary," as well as a drink named after her, "Res Mary." The drink, served at Chet's Melody Lounge, located across the street from the cemetery, consists of vodka and tomato juice. The late Chet Prusinski, who was the owner of Chet's, claimed Mary stopped in one evening and had a drink with him–a Res Mary, of course.

Address: **Resurrection Cemetery**
7201 Archer Ave.
Justice, IL

Directions: Take I-55 west to Hwy. 43. Go south on Hwy. 43 to 79th St. and turn right. Enter Justice and continue to Archer Ave. Turn right on Archer. Resurrection Cemetery is the second cemetery on the right.

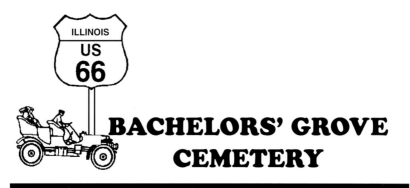

BACHELORS' GROVE CEMETERY

Bachelors' Grove Cemetery has the reputation of being the most haunted site in the Chicago area, and with all the haunted sites in Chicago, that is quite a reputation. The site became a graveyard in 1864 in an area settled by German immigrants. Since they were predominantly unmarried men, the area became known as Bachelors' Grove.

Today the area is the Rubio Woods Forest Preserve, near the Chicago suburb of Midlothian. The last burial took place in 1965 and the cemetery is now a monument to neglect and abuse. Weeds are knee-high. Gravestones have been stolen, knocked over, and spray painted. Graves have been opened and vandalized. Perhaps their desecration is the cause of the more than 100 paranormal incidents reported here, including ghost lights, voices and apparitions.

One of these apparitions is that of a farm house that appears and disappears randomly. Those who have seen it describe a white house with porch pillars, a swing and a soft light burning in the window.

Past the fence surrounding the cemetery is a small lagoon that borders the turnpike. This was once a popular dumping ground for Chicago gangsters and many bodies were found floating here, so it isn't surprising that the pond is said to be haunted. However, the apparitions seen here are not the victims of gangsters. A two-headed creature has been reported near the pond on many occasions. And even more often are

Bachelors' Grove Cemetery

reports of an old farmer who was pulled into the water by his plow horse in the 1870s. The horse was drowned by the weight of the plow and took the farmer under the water with him. Two forest rangers spotted the farmer guiding the horse and plow more than 100 years later.

Other ghosts inside the cemetery range from the image of monks to the spirit of a glowing yellow man. The most famous is White Lady. She is said to be the ghost of a woman buried in the cemetery next to her young son. She has been seen on nights of the full moon, wandering the cemetery with her baby in her arms.

Even the turnpike near the cemetery is said to be haunted. For a number of years witnesses have reported phantom cars that disappear along the road. One couple even had an auto accident with a car that vanished before their eyes, leaving their own vehicle untouched, despite the sounds of bending metal and breaking glass.

This cemetery is the most popular spot for ghost hunting that we've found. There are so many stories of this haunt that they begin to contradict each other. We spoke to one couple who have spent several family outings at the cemetery and while one was doubting the existence of the farm house, the other stated that not only had her young niece seen the house, she had been in it! Others claim that while the cemetery is in a forest preserve, you will never see animals or even insects inside its gates. However, on one trip to the cemetery, Barbara Huyser reports having seen a fawn calmly enjoying the afternoon sun, and on our trip we batted plenty of mosquitoes.

No two people seem to have the same experience at Bachelors' Grove and it appears unlikely that anyone has had the same experience twice. Once, when Barbara Huyser was at the cemetery she was speaking into a tape recorder. When she later played the tape back, there was a point where her voice was drowned out by the sound of a passing truck. However, she doesn't remember hearing a truck while she was in the cemetery. In fact, the sound of traffic from the street is completely muffled by the surrounding forest. She'd heard about the phantom cars though, and with that in mind she's returned in an attempt to pick up the sound again, but with no luck.

In only one area were we able to gain a consensus from nearly everyone we spoke to: ghost photos. Shoot a roll of film in Bachelors' Grove Cemetery and you will, more often than not, find some sort of anomaly in the developed pictures. Streaks of light, balls of light, even apparitions give credence to the claim that this cemetery is haunted.

Address: **Bachelors' Grove Cemetery**
Midlothian, Illinois

Directions: Take I-94 south to I-57, then south to Hwy 83 (147th Street), exit 350. Travel west to Cicero Ave. (Hwy. 50). Turn right and travel to Midlothian Turnpike. Turn west to the Rubio Woods Forest Preserve. The parking lot is on the north side of the street. The path to the cemetery is not easy to see, but if you cross the street and walk west 50 feet or so, you will see the chained-off path. The entrance to the cemetery is one quarter mile down the path.

COUNTRY HOUSE

The Country House, located in a quiet suburban neighborhood, was built in the 1820s as a tavern and store, with apartments for the owners upstairs. Through the years it has also been a speakeasy, a bar and a store. The roadhouse-style building now houses a restaurant and bar on the first floor with the upstairs used as office and storage space. Although there may be other ghosts haunting the property, the most famous spirit associated with the Country House is a female customer from the late 1950s.

The young woman, beautiful, blonde and in her late twenties, was a regular customer and one afternoon stopped by with her small daughter in tow. According to accounts, she was having an affair with the bartender and decided to leave after they got into a fight. Within half a mile of the restaurant her car hit a tree. The child survived, but the mother was killed. Whether it was an accident or suicide no one knows for sure.

Nothing happened to indicate a ghostly presence until the Regnery brothers, David and Patrick, took ownership of the building in 1974 and started renovating. One morning, David was in the kitchen with a carpenter. When he asked the carpenter if he wanted a beer, six shutters on the window opened up simultaneously. They both decided to have a drink elsewhere.

That was just the beginning. Slamming doors, the jukebox suddenly playing, thermostats resetting mysteriously, and sounds of a crying baby soon followed. One of her favorite pranks is to call out the names of customers who have been

*Country House
Restaurant*

waiting for a table. When they get to the hostess desk they discover their name hadn't been announced— not by a human that is!

In the summer of 1997, a carpenter remodeling the men's bathroom encountered the apparition of the pretty ghost. While working late at night when the restaurant was closed, he heard the jukebox start to play and went to check on it. When he came out of the washroom, he turned toward the bar and noticed a young woman with blonde hair standing by the jukebox. He had blocked open the door to let the sawdust go out, so he thought she had just walked in. Before he had a chance to explain that the Country House wasn't opened for business, he realized that from the hem of her dress down, there were no legs or feet–just air! She looked his way, then turned and moved down the bar. He crept around the corner of the bar a few minutes later, but she had vanished.

If the Country House's spirit limits herself to such harmless pranks, she will continue to be welcomed.

Address: **Country House**
          241 West 55th Street
          Clarendon Hills, IL

Phone: (630) 325-1444

Hours: Mon.-Thurs. 11:00 am - 1:00 am, Fri.-Sat. 11:00 am - 2:00 am, Sun. Noon-10:00 pm

Directions: On I-55, take Route 83 north to the 55th Street exit. Turn right (heading west) at the stoplight and travel three blocks.

RIALTO SQUARE THEATER

The Rialto Square Theater in Joliet opened in 1926 as a "palace for the people." It is still rated as one of the most beautiful theaters in the country. The inner lobby is styled after the Hall of Mirrors in the Palace of Versailles. The dome in the rotunda is reminiscent of the Pantheon in Rome and holds one of the largest, hand-cut crystal chandeliers in the country. Perhaps it's this dramatic beauty that drew the spirit of a beautiful young woman to the place.

Many people have felt her presence. At least two have seen her. One engineer described an icy coldness wash over him suddenly, which he believes was an encounter with the ghost. Others have heard strange noises and voices, have had objects moved from one place to another and have been brushed by a cold breeze as if someone had just rushed past them.

One employee of the Rialto, Goldie Groves, has a better rapport than most people can claim to have with a ghost. She believes she is more in tune to spirits due to a near death experience of her own. She's been working at the Rialto for eleven years and first encountered the ghost not long after she started. It was her first time working late at night. She was in the auditorium, walking down aisle four, and saw a cream-colored, hazy light at the Barton Grande organ. Out of the cloud a figure appeared and seemed to be floating around the organ. Goldie could see the figure was a woman. As Goldie focused on the woman's face, she noticed that the woman was young, late

Rialto Square Theater

twenties or early thirties, very pretty, and definitely not of this world.

Over the years, Goldie has had many encounters and knows when the ghost is around. She began calling the spirit Rachel. Once, when she was sitting with a co-worker, they felt an icy finger jab them both simultaneously. Goldie took it in stride and said, "Go bother the stage hands, Rachel."

Very clearly she heard the spirit reply, "My name is not Rachel; it's Raquel."

In turn, the spirit calls Goldie, who is half Cherokee, "Injun." The two seem to have a friendly relationship. Raquel has even helped Goldie find things she'd misplaced. However, even Goldie doesn't know why Raquel is at the Rialto, how long she's been there or where she comes from. Is she an actress from the past who never got a chance? A patron of the arts? All Goldie knows for sure is that Raquel loves the musicals performed at the Rialto. She shows up for every one.

Address: **Rialto Square Theater**
15 E. Van Buren
Joliet, IL 60432
Phone: (815) 726-7171

Please call for performance times and ticket information.

Directions: From I-55 entering Joliet, turn left on Hwy. 30 heading southeast for about six miles to the theater.

SPRINGFIELD THEATRE CENTRE

A good theater ghost should be dramatic. He should never miss his cues and he should create in his audience a willing suspension of disbelief. Joe Neville, the ghost of the Springfield Theatre Centre in Springfield, definitely fills the bill.

Acting may always have been a passion for Joe. It seemed to come to him easily. He passed himself off as an experienced actor who had performed across Europe, but no one is really sure this is true. His boss thought he was a loyal employee, until he was caught embezzling. Even after his death in 1951, when his will was published, the city learned that he left valuable items he didn't own–such as castles in Europe–to his friends in Springfield. Maybe Joe even had himself fooled.

He was to act in "Mr. Barry's Etchings." On the eve of opening night he learned through a friend his embezzlement had been discovered and he was to be arrested the following day. Either Joe couldn't handle going to jail, or he didn't want his opening night ruined. After the final dress rehearsal, Joe went home and took his life with a handful of pain killers, followed up with fish tank cleaner.

Even death could not keep Joe from the theater. The theory is that he is still waiting for his opening night. Whatever the reason, he has made so many appearances in so many ways that he is generally accepted as a part of the Springfield Theatre. Everyone seems to have a "Joe story."

Bart Gonterman, an actor and member of the Theatre

Guild, recalls the recent opening night of "Charlotte's Web" when he was acting as assistant director and stage manager. Part of his job was to walk through the building after the show to ensure that everything was closed and lights were off. He took a roundabout route, ending up turning off the back scene shop lights last, leaving him to exit the theater in darkness, except for the ghost light (a small lamp without a shade) on the stage. Since the light was behind him he could see his shadow in front of him as he walked out. About halfway out he saw a second shadow cross his own. He turned instantly and saw no one. He was alone—except perhaps for Joe.

Joe has many ways of making himself known. People working in the box office have seen the heavy theater doors swing open by themselves. Another Guild member brought in a class for a tour. The kids began asking about the ghost and the woman finally admitted she didn't really believe in Joe. At that precise moment all the lights in the theater went out. It seems Joe was trying very hard to convince her. While preparing a set one day, a man working on a ladder suddenly watched his scissors fall apart in his hand. One blade fell and impaled itself in the stage floor, directly at her feet.

Managing director Rebecca Sykes feels it's hard for anyone to doubt Joe's existence. Talk about him and he'll show up. Talk badly about him and he'll show up angry. While testing lights one day, a group of women were talking about Joe as a ladies' man, saying he'd sure get a kick out of seeing so many women on stage. Suddenly the piano player came up from the basement screaming, saying a chill just overtook her. As she reached the stage a heavy length of chain fell from the rafters, landing at her feet. There had been no chains used in the theater for years. No one knows where this one came from.

Rebecca said she recently saw Joe herself. She was working in the office above the theater where a large window overlooks the stage and any sound from the stage can be heard. She was talking on the phone, looking out the window at the stage. No one else was in the theater and the only light was the ghost light. In mid-sentence she paused as she tried to believe what she was seeing. Someone stepped out on the stage and walked behind the ghost light. It might have been someone who

Dressing room at Springfield Theatre–one of Joe's favorite haunts

just slipped into the theater, but any typical movement should have made a sound. The figure was completely silent. Rebecca had the sense that the figure was not quite real.

In 1996 the theater group decided to perform the fateful "Mr. Barry's Etchings," which had not been staged since Joe's death. They chose Halloween for the opening night. All the performers were nervous, wondering what Joe would do. Everyone was surprised that nothing happened–until they checked the camera. Three times they attempted to film the performance and three times the camera shut itself off.

The Springfield Theatre Guild may make "Mr. Barry's Etchings" an annual tribute to Joe and they will probably choose Halloween for the performance date. If you enjoy a good scare, you may want to drop in.

Address: **Springfield Theatre Centre**
101 East Lawrence
Springfield, IL 62704

Phone: (217) 523-0878

Hours: Call for a schedule of performances.

Directions: From I-55, take the Springfield (6th Street) exit. Travel south on 6th to Grand Avenue and turn left. Travel five blocks to Spring Street, turn right. Take Spring to Lawrence and turn right.

DANA-THOMAS HOUSE

If you visit the Dana-Thomas House, just down the street from the Springfield Theatre, you will not hear a peep about ghosts. However, many visitors to this historic site will tell you they have indeed felt a presence.

No one has identified the presence but the home had few former residents. The most likely might be Susan Lawrence Dana, a Springfield socialite. Susan once used the house for lavish entertaining. Her guests included governors, state politicians, and other members of local society. Her life was far from one big party, however. Susan had her share of tragedy. While her first marriage was happy and lasted seventeen years, her two children died in infancy and, on the heels of her husband's death, she lost her father. Her second marriage was only a year old when her husband died unexpectedly and suddenly. A third marriage ended in divorce.

Perhaps it was a search for comfort or answers that triggered Susan's interest in metaphysical and mystical religious groups. Spiritualism was popular in the 1920s. Mediums had popped up like weeds, ready to communicate with those who had passed to the other side. Such groups met at Susan's home. She even founded her own group–the Lawrence Center for Constructive Thought. Susan died in 1946. As she may not have found answers or comfort, her spirit may still reside at her old home.

One visitor, Stephanie Bailey, remembered taking her

Dana-Thomas House

class of school kids through the home on a tour at Christmas time. "I felt a cold rush of air, as if something had walked past me, brushing my arm. I looked around, but no one was there. Whatever it was, it gave me chills inside and out. I tried not to react to the house because I didn't want the kids to get scared. I did not feel comfortable until we were out of there."

Other visitors to the house have had similar experiences. No one we spoke to was quite sure what they were experiencing—the spirit of Susan Lawrence or just a spiritual sense. Whatever it was, they knew it was other-worldly.

Address:	**Dana-Thomas House**
	301 E. Lawrence Ave.
	Springfield, IL 62703
Phone:	(217) 782-6773
Hours:	Wednesday - Sunday 9:00 am - 4:00 pm

Directions: From I-55, take the Springfield exit marked "6th Street." Travel south on 6th Street to Grand Ave., turn left. Travel approximately five blocks to Spring Street and turn right. Take Spring to Lawrence, turn right. The Dana-Thomas House is on the left side of the road about 2 blocks down.

ABRAHAM LINCOLN HOME

Springfield, Illinois — — — — — — — — — — — —

In 1844 the Abraham Lincoln family moved into their new home on the corner of Eighth and Jackson Streets in Springfield. It was the only home they ever owned and they resided there until they left for the White House in 1861. The time spent there was absorbed in starting their family (Robert had been born only six months before), making improvements to the house, and Lincoln's law career. Although they lost a son in 1850, compared to the rest of her life those were probably happy, peaceful days for Mary Lincoln. This may explain why there are so many rumors that her spirit is still in this house.

When we visited the Lincoln home, now a National Historic Site and run by the National Park Service, we set a trio of park rangers into fits of laughter when we asked about the ghost. No, they assured us, there are not and never have been any ghosts in the Lincoln house. People who believe they have seen strange things in the house have really been seeing tour guides entertaining themselves. The rocking chair that rocks by itself, for example, was really being rocked by an employee with a string. We asked others associated with the Lincoln Home and received similar assurances. We looked at each other and shrugged. This place must not be haunted after all, if the people who work here say it isn't.

Troy Taylor, author of *Haunted Springfield* and other books about haunted sites, claims that a lot of sites that are said to *not* be haunted sure seem to have plenty of ghosts!

Abraham Lincoln Home

As it turns out, former employees are quite ready to talk about strange happenings in the Lincoln Home. They spoke on one occasion to the State Journal Register, and yes, they did report seeing Lincoln's favorite chair rocking. They also saw other pieces of furniture and toys show up in different rooms of the house at different times. Candles, which had never been lighted, have been found burned down.

One employee remembers a time she was in the house alone, all set to rearrange the furniture in Mary Lincoln's bedroom. She felt someone tap her on the shoulder. When she turned around, no one was there. She left the furniture alone.

A former guide was working at the front door one afternoon and heard the sound of piano music coming from the parlor. She turned to stop whoever was playing it, but there was no one around. Another guide reported strange feelings and the touch of invisible hands. Even visitors have written about strange occurrences. One reports having seen an apparition in the parlor that he believed to be Mary Lincoln.

So when you visit the Lincoln Home, take the advice of the scoffers– don't believe everything you hear. Keep your eyes open, there's no telling what you might see!

Address: **The Abraham Lincoln Home**
Corner of 8th and Jackson Streets
Springfield, IL 62701

Phone: (217) 492-4241

Hours: Note: Admission is free, but tickets must be obtained at the Visitor Center at 426 S. 7th St. before touring the house. The Center is one block west of the Lincoln Home. Mail should be addressed to the administration offices at 413 S. 8th St.

Directions: From I-55, take the Springfield exit marked "6th Street." Travel south on 6th Street to Grand Avenue, turn left. Travel approximately five blocks to Spring Street and turn right. Take Spring to Lawrence, turn right. Travel east on Lawrence to 7th Street and turn left. Travel 3 blocks to the corner of 8th and Jackson.

THE INN AT 835

You might have had a hard time finding a successful business woman around the turn of the century. In Springfield, however, you would have certainly found Bell Miller. In fact, you might still find her today, or at least her spirit, at the Inn at 835.

Bell plunged into the business world as a florist in the early 1890s. Only in her twenties, she was savvy enough to target a "High Society" clientele. She became a florist to the Springfield elite and her business flourished. As Bell became more successful in her trade, she decided to diversify. Working with noted architect George Helmle, she developed a building of six luxury apartments at 835 South Second Street. This soon became one of the most prestigious addresses in Springfield.

Bell's classic revival apartment building still exists today and is listed on the National Register of Historic Places. Court Conn purchased the building in 1994 and transformed four of the luxury apartments into seven guest rooms, named after the very flowers that gave Bell her start. Although Court has never seen Bell for himself, he's heard enough stories about her activities to concede that her spirit may well reside at the Inn today.

Don Bailey, who has lived in his apartment at the Inn both before and since the remodeling, has had many experiences with Bell. The first was not long before the remodeling began. His wife, Velma, was out for the evening and Don was home alone, relaxing and listening to some classical music. Out of

The Inn at 835

nowhere, a warm, friendly voice said, "Well, hello there." Startled, Don jumped up, looked around, and saw he was still alone. When he checked the hall and found no one there, he wondered if he was just hearing things. But the voice sure sounded real. With no explanation at hand, he tried to put the experience out of his mind.

He was successful for about two weeks. Then one evening he and Velma had just come home from work to find a book, *My Sister Eileen,* lying on the floor in the middle of the room. The book had been in a rather tightly packed bookcase against a wall. It was unlikely that it had fallen out and even if it had, would it have landed in the middle of the room? Neither could explain how the book ended up on the floor; they returned it to the shelf. A week later they found the same book, back in the middle of the floor. Remembering the voice he's heard, Don was already wondering if they had a ghost on their hands and decided to try an experiment. He left the book open on a table, taking note of the pages on top and wondering if the ghost might turn them. Unfortunately, Bell did not take the bait.

About a month later, in late November, Don was trimming the Christmas tree in the living room, which is at the front of the building. Velma was in back in the kitchen. Suddenly he heard that friendly voice again: "Well I see we're getting ready for the holidays." Knowing he'd find no one, he looked around the room and checked the hall. Velma, who was still in the kitchen, had heard nothing.

Over the New Year's holiday, Don and Velma were entertaining friends from out of town. When the two couples sat down to dinner, one of the guests noticed the wallpaper was coming off the wall. Don looked and sure enough, about six inches of paper had rolled down from the top of the wall. He realized he'd have to take care of that quickly, before the paper was torn, but he never got the chance. The next morning his guest looked up at the wall and said, "My, you took care of that paper fast." To everyone's surprise, the paper was perfectly back in place. Neither he nor Velma had made the repair. It had to be the ghost.

Lately Velma has heard someone checking the contents of a crystal candy dish. She can hear the "ting" of the lid being lifted and replaced. Both of them occasionally catch a glimpse of a figure passing a doorway. Then there's the elevator, which takes its passengers where it pleases regardless of which button they press. Court has had it inspected and serviced several times. The diagnosis is always the same–there's nothing wrong with it. It either has a mind of its own, or an invisible operator.

Bell's spirit is obviously playful and friendly. She seems to want only to remind everyone of her existence. This was her building after all, and as a true businesswoman she must oversee its daily operations.

Address: **The Inn at 835**
              835 South Second Street
              Springfield, IL 62704

Phone: (217) 523-4466 or (888) 217-4835
              Visit our site: www.innat835.com

Directions: From I-55, exit on South Grand Avenue. Travel west to Second Street. Turn right (north) and go one block to Canedy. The inn is on the corner of Second and Canedy.

Missouri

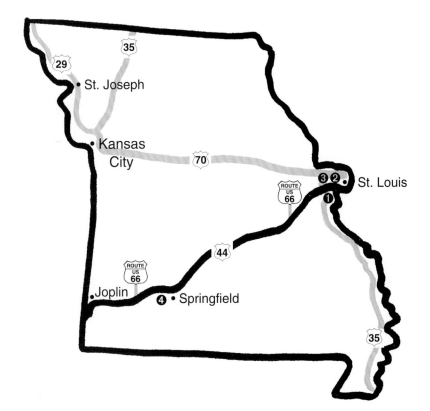

❶ **St. Louis:**
  Lemp Mansion
  Bissell Mansion Restaurant
❷ **Bridgeton:** *Payne-Gentry House*
❸ **St. Charles:** *Goldenrod Showboat*
❹ **Springfield:**
  Walnut Street Inn
  The Landers Theatre
  Phelps Grove Park

LEMP MANSION

The Lemp Mansion in St Louis, is a house haunted by great tragedy. Built in the early 1860s, it was purchased by brewery baron William J. Lemp, who turned it into a Victorian showplace. It never quite made it as a happy home, however. When Frederick Lemp, William's son and heir, died mysteriously in 1901, William never got over it. Three years later he shot himself through the heart in his office at the mansion. In the 1920s, William's daughter, Elsa, committed suicide. In 1922, due to prohibition, the Lemp brewery was sold at auction for less than one tenth of its former value. After presiding over the sale, the junior Lemp shot himself in the same office in which his father had died. William's brother, Charles, stayed in the house after the suicide until 1949, when he too died of a self-inflicted gunshot wound. Of William's children, only Edwin Lemp died of natural causes at the age of ninety.

After Charles' death, the house and its artifacts were sold at auction and the mansion became a boarding or "flop" house. With such a history, there is no wonder this house is haunted. Paul Pointer, whose family has owned the Lemp Mansion since 1975, reports that psychics who have been to the mansion have blamed the sightings and other poltergeist activities on the house itself.

The most common sighting is of the so-called monkey child. A number of people have reported seeing a deformed child in the upper floors of the mansion, which used to be the family bedrooms and now serves as a bed and breakfast. Back in the Lemps' time there was a rumor of such a child, possibly an

Lemp Mansion

illegitimate child of one of the Lemp boys–Frederick, William, or Charles–and one of the servants. In those days a deformed child was something you kept hidden away. To add credence to the rumor, there is an unmarked child's grave at the Lemp mausoleum in Calvary Cemetery. Since the last member of the Lemp family died in 1970, this story will always be supposition.

In 1982 Paul Pointer's father received a strange letter from a man in Alabama who had lived in a basement apartment in the mansion in the 1950s. The man described the house with great detail and accuracy as he relayed an account of his own encounter with a spirit. He'd been walking from the bathroom to his rooms late one night, only to be stopped short at the stairs by the appearance of a ghost. He described the ghost as a man, short and slender, with small features and dark hair combed straight back. He was well-dressed and wore highly-polished shoes, which stood out against the red-painted floor. At first the man panicked and turned to flee, but something told him not to show fear. He turned back an instant later and the specter was gone. The man believed this was the ghost of Charles Lemp.

Paul had seen the letter and found it interesting, but thought nothing more of it until several years later. While he was working in the restaurant, a waiter, who was downstairs punching his time card, came running up saying he had seen a ghost. The man was obviously shaken, his face pale and ashen, so Paul and others tried to calm him down by asking him to describe exactly what he had seen. The first thing he mentioned was the shiny shoes. There was no chance that the waiter knew of the letter Paul's father had received describing the same ghost.

In addition to sightings, plenty of mischievous activities take place in the house. Equipment and tools are moved, doors open and close by themselves, and a piano plays itself constantly. Paul set a bottle of wine down once only to see it spontaneously explode. Upstairs in the bedrooms one can often hear the thud of someone kicking the bottom of the door. Open the door and no one will be there, but some believe it is the ghost of the deformed child trying to gain admittance.

There are many opportunities to visit the spirits of the Lemp Mansion. The Lemp Mansion Restaurant takes up the first floor, or if you wish to see the entire house in all its splendor, you can schedule a tour. The Pointers also host a murder mystery dinner theater with audience participation every Friday and Saturday night. However, if you really want to immerse yourself in the poltergeist activities, spend the night at the Lemp Mansion–if you dare!

Address:	**Lemp Mansion**
	3322 DeMenil Place
	St. Louis, MO 63118
Phone:	(314) 664-8024
Hours:	Mon. - Fri. 11:00 - 2:30, Thurs. - Sat. 5:30 - 10:00
	Sunday 11:30 - 8:00

Directions: From the Arch, follow I-55 south 3 miles to Arsenal (exit 206C). Turn right and travel 1 block to Lemp Ave. Turn left and travel 3 blocks to Utah Street. Travel left on Utah for 2 blocks and turn right at DeMenil Place.

BISSELL MANSION RESTAURANT

St. Louis, Missouri

In direct contrast to the Lemp Mansion, another St. Louis haunt, the Bissell Mansion Restaurant, was a happy home. The spirits here seem determined to see that it stays that way.

The Bissell Mansion, the oldest brick house in St. Louis, was built in 1823 by Captain Lewis Bissell, a prominent St. Louis resident. He was in his early thirties with an impressive military career and a great deal of land in the St. Louis area, 1500 acres of which became known as Bissell's Point. He built his home on a hill overlooking the Mississippi River. From this site, he could also watch St. Louis grow as he sold his land a parcel at a time, making his investment a very wise one.

In 1821, the Captain married Mary Woodbridge. She died ten years later and he married again in 1837, this time to Mary Jane Douglas. Bissell died in his home in 1868 at the age of 79. Although he'd lived a good and full life, it seems that he is not ready to leave.

Today the old mansion is a restaurant and dinner theater, and it may be the locale of Captain Bissell's spirit who stands guard outside his former home. Barbara Schepker of the Bissell Restaurant says that a group of psychics came in one night for dinner, felt the spirits and asked if they could investigate. They say there is a male spirit who stays outside and is very protective of the house. Inside is a female spirit who seems to spread an aura of tranquility wherever she appears. A waiter who saw her for the first time was surprised,

Bissell Mansion Restaurant and Mystery Dinner Theater

but definitely not frightened. He saw her walking up the stairs in a white, flowing gown. When she sensed his presence, she turned her head and gave him a smile over her shoulder.

Customers and employees alike have felt the presence of the spirits and agree–there is something warm and comforting about them. What wonderful spirits to have around! Maybe the captain, who played such a large part in the building of St. Louis, simply can't bear to leave it.

Address: **Bissell Mansion Restaurant**
4426 Randall Place
St. Louis, MO 63107

Phone: (314) 533-9830

Hours: Lunch: Tues.-Fri. from 11:30-2:30. Participatory Mystery Theater: Fri. and Sat. at 7:00 and Sun. at 2:00 includes a 5 course dinner and wine.

Directions: From I-55, take I-70 west to the Grand Avenue exit. Turn left on Grand. At the next stoplight, turn left onto Blair. When you come to the red brick water tower in the middle of the road, go three-quarters of the way around it, and turn right onto Bissell. At the dead end, turn right onto Randall–the mansion is on the left.

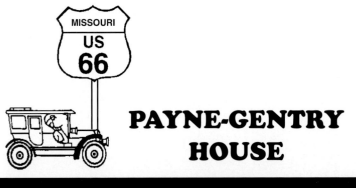

PAYNE-GENTRY HOUSE

The Payne-Gentry House is a Victorian cottage built in 1870 and owned by only one family. Yet it has been said that this house is occupied by 23 separate entities. Where did they come from?

Aldridge Payne was a merchant who owned stores in both St. Louis and Memphis. This house was the Payne family's summer home. When Aldridge Payne died in 1874, Mary Elizabeth chose to make this her permanent home with her five-year-old daughter, Mary Lee, while her son went off to college and medical school. Upon the son's return he opened his office in the house and practiced medicine there for 17 years.

Anne Theil, a member of the Bridgeton Historical Society, believes this may be the source of some of the spirits. This seems to be a logical conclusion considering the calm history of the house and the fact that, in those days, doctors lost about as many patients as they saved.

During evening tours of the house, its not unusual to see members of the group looking around for a dog. Apparently there is a canine spirit who lingers near a tree in the yard. People feel him brush their legs, but when they bend over to pet him, they find nothing but air.

Other strange things happen here. Doors open and close by themselves and people have reported seeing apparitions. The most common sighting is of a woman in a white tea dress. She is believed to be Mary Lee, who died while giving birth to

Payne-Gentry House
Photo courtesy Walt Pfeiffer

her second child, a daughter who also died.

Anne Thiel has never seen Mary Lee herself, but a tour guide once told her of his sighting. He was sitting on the back porch when he saw a woman in a white dress walk up to the front door. Assuming he had a visitor, he got up and entered the house from the back. When he got to the door, the woman was nowhere to be seen.

Address: **Payne-Gentry House**
4211 Fee Road
Bridgeton, MO 63044

Phone: (314) 739-6149 or schedule a tour of this and other St. Louis haunted houses by contacting BKS Management at (314) 940-1599.

Hours: The house is open from 1:00 - 4:00 pm on the first and third Sundays–Feb. to Nov.

Directions: From St. Louis, take I-70 west to North Lindbergh Blvd (US 67), heading northeast. Turn left on Natural Bridge Rd. (Hwy. 115). Travel approximately half a mile to Fee Rd. Turn right.

GOLDENROD SHOWBOAT

The *Goldenrod* showboat is the last of the original showboats to travel the Mississippi. Its charm inspired Edna Ferber to write the book *Showboat.* From the book came the play and then the movie. One thing you won't find in any version of *Showboat* is a ghost, but you might find one on the *Goldenrod!*

The staff of the *Goldenrod* call the ghost Victoria, but they don't know her real name. After several encounters with the spirit, a curious employee did some research into the history of the boat. She found that around the turn of the century, an employee of the showboat was raising his daughter on board, and when she became old enough, she acted in some of the productions. One night, while docked in St. Louis, they had a fight and the daughter left the boat to cool off. She was brutally attacked by a band of "river rats" and dumped into the river. She was found in the river the next morning. Her spirit wasn't seen until after her father's death; she was wearing the same red dress she'd died in.

When the *Goldenrod* was brought to St. Charles to be docked permanently, it was completely restored to its original glory. That's when the staff of the *Goldenrod* first encountered Victoria. An employee was installing stair lights in the balcony of the theater when he heard lively music coming from the banquet room. He went to the banquet room to check it out and found it empty. Steve Powell of the St. Charles Convention and Visitors' Bureau was instrumental in bringing the *Goldenrod*

Goldenrod Showboat

to St. Charles and supervised the restoration. He heard of many strange happenings during that time. When a contractor came in to service the generator he watched in amazement as a mirror flew off the wall when the boat was perfectly calm. When the general manager locked up the gate at night, he saw a face peer out the window. Steve heard these reports and began to wonder what was going on.

At first, most employees tried to explain things away. "It's an old boat, of course there's funny noises," or "a lot of people work here, things get misplaced." But when it happened again and again, they started to wonder. Lights that were turned off came back on. Doors that had been left locked were found open.

Some experiences however, simply defy explanation. One employee stopped by the boat one afternoon to pick up her schedule. She found the doors open, but all the lights and the PA system turned off. She went through the lobby, box office and manager's office in the dark without finding a soul. Yet, people should have been there working. She decided she didn't really want to investigate further and turned to leave. Just as she did, the lights flashed on and music started playing. She left the boat at a run.

She later asked the manager and staff why they'd left so early that day and got an answer that baffled her. They swore they were there. No one had left early; they were all on board. Yet she knew there had been no one around when she arrived.

Victoria had little sympathy for a chef who was having a bad night and made the mistake of cursing the boat. Immediately pots and pans began crashing about the room, knives flew off the wall and food was flying everywhere. Nobody had touched anything, the river was calm, and nothing had happened in any other room.

The employees of the *Goldenrod* accept and respect Victoria. She's not just the spirit of the *Goldenrod*, but the spirit of a bygone time that the *Goldenrod* represents. Many believe she protects the boat and keeps them safe. So many have felt her presence in one way or another that they are certain she is real—and they invite you to come and meet her.

Address: **Goldenrod Showboat**
1000 Riverside Drive
St. Charles, MO 63301

Phone: (314) 946-2020

Hours: The *Goldenrod* has both matinee and evening performances. Call for times and prices, or call the Greater St. Charles Convention and Visitors' Bureau at 800-366-2427.

Directions: I-70 west to the Fifth Street exit. Turn right at Booneslick Road. When you cross South Main Street the *Goldenrod* will be straight ahead toward the river.

WALNUT STREET INN

This three-story Victorian bed and breakfast was built in the mid-1890s by Charles McCann. According to the journal that Charles kept, his house cost him $6,000. He was especially pleased, he noted, with the 20 iron Corinthian columns, which are still standing.

Because the prominent McCann and his wife, Katherine, liked to entertain they used the entire downstairs for their parties. The oak floors that their guests danced on are still in excellent condition, and the leaded glass windows that Katherine peeked through to see her callers arriving, are now kept polished by Paula Blankenship, the innkeeper. Four original light fixtures remain in the foyer, dining room, gift shop, and Craver Room.

On the west side of the Walnut Street Inn, the carriage entrance used by the McCanns is still in use. In 1992 the carriage house, complete with horse stalls and carriage master's quarters, was renovated into four guest rooms.

Shadows of the past are visible on the grounds that surround the Walnut Street Inn. Among the towering walnut and sycamore trees is a rare German linden tree. Speculation is that it might have been purchased from one of the many drummers who traveled the roads after the Civil War.

The Rosen Room's private bath boasts the original porcelain fixtures and built-in cabinetry. The room also boasts of having its own ghost.

Although some of Paula's previous guests have felt a

Walnut Street Inn

"ghostly" presence, it wasn't until 1998 that a gentleman staying in the Rosen Room saw the apparition. He was stretched out on his bed when he looked up and was startled to see a female sitting at a table against the wall. "Excuse me, this is my room," he said. The ghost turned to him and said, "No, this is *my* room." "He shook himself, thinking he was asleep," Paula explained. "Then she just disappeared."

When some of the staff at the Inn learned of the incident, they decided to use a Ouija board to attempt to communicate with the unexpected guest. They learned that she was probably in her 70s when she passed away and has stayed on to watch over the house. When you make reservations to stay at the Walnut Street Inn, be sure to request the Rosen Room. You'll sleep peacefully knowing you're being looked after.

Address:	**Walnut Street Inn**
	900 E. Walnut
	Springfield, MO 65806
Phone:	(800) 593-6346 or (417) 864-6346

Directions: From I-44 take U.S. Highway 65 South. Exit Chestnut Expressway, turn right to Sherman Avenue. Turn south (left) and go 4 blocks to Walnut Street. Turn west on Walnut.

THE
LANDERS THEATRE

The Landers Theatre has been operating almost continuously since it opened in 1909. It began as a live vaudeville house on the Orpheum Circuit and continued through 1919. Silent movies took over through the twenties and gradually the talkies moved in. It was closed for a short period in the mid-40s when World War Two left few people around to operate a theater, but it came back to life after the war ended and continued showing movies through the sixties. In 1970 the building was purchased by the Springfield Little Theater, who have been bringing live theatrical productions to the Landers ever since.

The building was designed and built by the famous architects, Carl and Robert Boller. They combined several architectural styles in the four-story building, including baroque, renaissance, and neo-classical. They also built in some special architectural fixtures that look like screaming devils that some believe are meant to ward off evil spirits. While there is no evidence that the Bollers added these features for any purpose other than design, the screaming devils might just be doing a darn good job. There may be spirits in the Landers Theatre, but they certainly aren't evil.

In fact there are many stories of spirits here, as might be expected in an old building where human emotion is part of the daily fare. People on the street in front of the building have reported seeing a figure of a man behind one of the fourth floor windows. He is described as very tall, with long blonde hair, wearing Elizabethan clothing. This side of the fourth floor used to be apartments, and for a time they had been used to house touring actors. Maybe this spirit is one of them. No one has ever seen him from inside the room, now a costume room, only from the street below.

The theater is also supposed to house the spirit of a mother and her child. People have said they've heard a child crying, followed by the sound of a mother comforting him to silence with coos and shushes. When they look around, no one is there.

The Landers Theatre

A third spirit comes from the twenties and the days of segregation. During that time the second mezzanine balcony was the "colored" balcony. The story is that a man had been knifed there and died. Now his spirit manifests itself as a green phosphorescent haze, which is about twenty degrees colder than the area around it.

While these are older stories and few people report experiencing them today, there are still spirits at the Landers that keep the current staff on their toes. They'll have a sense of someone following them or feel a tap on their shoulder when no one is there. Chuck Rogers, the scenic lighting designer and technical director, has been with the Springfield Little Theater for fifteen years. During the early part of his career he lived in one of the upstairs rooms. He was sleeping in his room one night when something woke him. He looked around the room and saw the shape of a person, silhouetted by the lights from the window behind. He couldn't make out any features–it was just a dark form. After a while he pushed the incident from his mind, but recently something happened that brought it back.

A group of people from the theater were playing with a Ouija board in the balcony one night and told Chuck they were contacted by a spirit from the theater. He said his name was Ned and that he spent his time in the boiler room. Chuck didn't think much of their experience at the time but he remembered it a few nights later when he was closing the theater after a show. The security system wasn't properly set so he went down to the basement to check it out. When he came back up he saw someone standing in the auditorium. Chuck asked if he could help the man, but got no response. "The theater is closed, " he said. "Is there something I can do for you?" As he moved closer, the man stepped around one of the columns and vanished. Chuck followed but couldn't find him.

He later told the Ouija board players about his experience and they set up the board again to find out who Chuck had seen. The planchette spelled out a description which they relayed to Chuck–a middle-aged man, just under six feet tall, a little heavyset, with shoulder length hair and a beard, both black mixed with grey. He had a big nose with fleshy lips and bushy eyebrows. It was the very man Chuck had seen. No one knows who this man is, but it seems the boiler room isn't his only haunt.

You may believe whatever you wish about Ouija boards and ghosts, but Chuck became a believer that night.

Address: **The Landers Theatre**
             311 E. Walnut St.
             Springfield, MO 65806

Phone: (417) 869-3869

Directions: From I-44 take U.S. Highway 65 South. Exit Chestnut Expressway, turn right to Sherman Avenue. Turn south (left) and go 4 blocks to Walnut Street. Turn west on Walnut.

PHELPS GROVE PARK

The forty-four acres in Phelps Grove Park is a lovely place to take a coffee break, a picnic lunch or an evening walk. The park is equipped with baseball fields, barbeques, picnic tables, horseshoes and, of course, a ghost.

The park has in its past a number of incidents that might lend themselves to the spirit world. As early as 1812, a Kickapoo Indian settlement occupied the site. When the land belonged to John S. Phelps, the body of Union general Nathaniel Lyon was temporarily buried there until relatives could come from Connecticut to claim him.

As old as the park is, the spirit is relatively new, her death the result of an auto accident. Although no one has put a name to this spirit, it is not difficult to find someone who has heard of her, or knows the story behind her death. Supposedly, on the day of her wedding, she and her new husband were driving through the park and were killed in a crash.

Now the ghost of the bride appears beside the center of three bridges that lead to the park. Shelly Hale, who lives near the park, says she has seen the "bride ghost" many times. "She always appears in the evening and you can see her from the road. But, if you go down to where she's standing–she's gone."

Shelly saw the ghost for the first time with her four-year-old daughter who pointed out the bride. She stands near the bridge with her right hand on her hip and her left holding up the

The ghost is usually seen near this bridge in Phelps Grove Park.

hem of her long dress, as if she were about to take a step. Her long hair streams over her shoulders and you can see the detail of the lace in her white gown, train and veil. Where a face should be, there is simply darkness.

Since the spirit is unknown, no one can say why she lingers here, ready to take a step but never taking it.

Address: **Phelps Grove Park**
800-1200 E. Bennett
Springfield, MO

Directions: From I-44, take Glenstone south to East Bennett and turn right. The park ranges between the 800-1200 blocks of East Bennett.

Kansas, Oklahoma, Texas

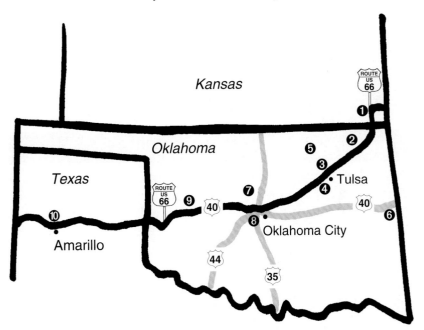

❶ **Baxter Springs, KS:** *Fort Blair*
❷ **Miami/Quapaw Area, OK:** *Spooklight*
❸ **Claremore, OK:** *Belvedere Mansion*
❹ **Tulsa, OK:**
    Brady Theater
    Gilcrease Museum
❺ **Pawhuska, OK:** *Constantine Theater*
❻ **Spiro, OK:** *Spiro Mounds*
❼ **Guthrie, OK:**
    Stone Lion Inn
    Gray Brothers Building
❽ **Oklahoma City, OK:** *Overholser Mansion*
❾ **Arapaho, OK:** *Arapaho Cemetery*
❿ **Amarillo, TX:** *The Nat*

FORT BLAIR

When the Historical Society in Baxter Springs decided to restore an old frontier fort, they had to purchase the homes currently occupying the site. They got a little something extra they hadn't bargained for–the ghost of a Buffalo Soldier!

How this man's spirit came to be in Baxter Springs is a matter of speculation that requires a look at the history of this area. The Territory of Kansas became a state three short months before the first shots of the Civil War were fired. More importantly, Kansas entered the Union as a "free state." That choice came after so many violent clashes between free-state and pro-slavery factions that the territory earned the nickname, "Bleeding Kansas." The Union army knew it hadn't quieted all the pro-slavers, so they established several forts in Kansas. These forts were the training ground for many Buffalo Soldiers–black soldiers of the Civil War.

The Confederacy was understandably annoyed that Kansas had become a free state. One confederate in particular, William Quantrill, took it personally. Quantrill had been causing havoc for years in neighboring Missouri with the declared goal of protecting that state from the Union hordes of Kansas. Even though the "Union hordes" of Kansas were too busy to bother much with Missouri, Quantrill's mind was made up. A visit from Quantrill has been described as wanton "murder, arson, robbery, pillage and inexcusable savagery." He was so uncontrollable he was an embarrassment to the Confederacy, who held chivalry and honor in high esteem.

Fortunately, the soldiers at Fort Blair were prepared. They held the fort and suffered few casualties. At that time Quantrill received word that a supply wagon was approaching. Such an easy mark was too much for him to resist. The raid left about 100 people dead, and apparently satisfied Quantrill. He left Fort Blair alone. All the bodies were brought to the fort and buried there. Not long after the raid, the Union army decided to abandon the fort but didn't want it to fall into the hands of the Confederacy. It was burned to the ground.

After the Civil war, the town of Baxter Springs grew. Houses were built over the site of the fort. In the 1990s the Historical Society began buying those houses. During negotiations one elderly resident, stated, "If you buy the house, the ghost goes with it." Phyllis Abbott, of the Historical Society, asked the woman what she meant. The woman meant a ghost. She described it as a dark man, wearing a military uniform. This sounded like the description of a soldier. The woman and her daughter swore the ghost occupied their house. He never caused any problems, he just showed up–a lot.

Phyllis asked other neighbors if they'd ever encountered anything. One described the Buffalo Soldier and another referred to a "dark presence." She also heard of a real estate agent who had been in the house a few years back when the family was considering selling. They said as the agent walked into one of the rooms, saw the ghost, turned and fled, never to return. The soldier might have been one of the few casualties from the Fort Blair attack or he might have been an escort for the supply wagon. Those were the only battles in the area.

The Historical Society plans to build a replica of the fort on its original site and open it to the public. All the houses on the site have been purchased and razed and the area is now under excavation. If we've learned anything from this trip, it's that renovation certainly stirs up ghosts. We're not sure if excavation has the same effect or not, but if there are any other spirits left from the ill-fated fort, the historical society may have their hands full.

Directions: The site is in Baxter Springs, KS. On Military (Route 66) between 6th and 7th Streets.

SPOOKLIGHT

If you spend a little time in northeastern Oklahoma, around the area of Miami or Quapaw, you will hear about Spooklight. Every local resident has either seen it themselves or knows someone who has. From the descriptions we hear, it is a ball of light, sometimes with a tail, sometimes completely round. It is seen in the evening, dancing across the horizon. If you approach, it recedes; if you back away, it moves toward you; and sometimes it simply hovers. One area resident said she went out to view Spooklight with her parents when she was a child and saw the ball of light flash right through their car.

No one seems to know what causes this mysterious light show. The Army Corps of Engineers studied the phenomenon in the 1940s and came up with no explanation. Since Spooklight has been haunting this area for more than a century, it's only natural that there are plenty of tales. We've heard two versions. One story states that Spooklight is the ghost of an Indian couple, while the other is that it is the ghost of a man looking for his wife and children, abducted by Indians. While these may be stories, the light itself is real. Plenty of people have seen it–they just don't know what it is.

Directions: Route 66 runs from Kansas straight through Miami and Quapaw. People have reported seeing Spooklight in all of these areas, but the best viewing is supposed to be one and one-half miles east of Quapaw on a bluff called Devil's Promenade near the Spring River.

BELEVEDERE MANSION

John M. Bayless was quite an important man in Claremore even before he decided to make the town his home. About the turn of the century, Bayless was a resident of Tulsa, where he earned his fortune through hard work and smart investments, some of which included building the town of Claremore. Two of his contributions to the town were the Opera House and the Sequoyah Hotel, considered to be among the finest in the territory. Afterward, Bayless decided to build his own home in Claremore and drew up the plans himself. Just as construction was about to start, Bayless died of complications from appendicitis in 1907.

His wife used John's plans to complete the three-story home, called Belevedere, and followed them to the letter, right down to the castle-like turrets. The family resided at Belevedere until the children had all established homes of their own. The mansion was sold about 1919 and converted into apartments. It has recently been restored to its old glory. You can take a tour of the old mansion and even spend the night if you choose, but keep your eyes open for the ghost of John Bayless when you head up to the third floor.

Mr. Bayless insisted that the third floor be used for family enjoyment and social occasions. While it may have changed during its days as an apartment building, today the third floor is a wide open ballroom with pillars bearing the weight of the ceiling. The figure of a man was spotted behind one of those

Third floor ballroom at Belvedere Mansion

pillars by one of the docents. She also saw the man vanish. Since John Bayless never got the chance to see this house during his lifetime, could he have decided to spend his afterlife there? Maybe you should see for yourself!

Address:	**Belvedere Mansion** 121 N. Chickasaw Claremore, OK 74017
Phone:	Rogers County Historical Society (918) 342-1127
Hours:	Thursday-Saturday 10:00 am to 4:00 pm

Directions: From Route 66 head southeast into Claremore. Turn right on Will Rogers Boulevard, travel approximately 5 blocks and turn left on Chickasaw. The mansion is across the street from the Carriage House Bed & Breakfast.

BRADY THEATER

The Brady Theater in downtown Tulsa is a great place to attend a concert, the ballet or a play. You can also rent a reception room for a party or meeting, although you might want to save a seat for a famous, unexpected guest–the spirit of Enrico Caruso, who haunts this historic building.

As the story goes, Caruso's death in 1921 was triggered by his stop in Tulsa. The day of his performance he went out for a ride to the oil wells around Sapulpa in an open touring car. It

Brady Theater

began raining, and to make matters worse the car broke down. Worried about missing his show, Caruso began walking back toward Tulsa in the rain. Somewhere along the way he caught a ride and arrived at the theater just in time to go on stage. Caruso reportedly gave the best performance of his life that evening. Unfortunately he came down with pneumonia and never fully recovered. A year later he died, but his spirit is spotted from time to time at the Brady.

Caruso is not the only spirit at the theater. The Brady has a chilling story in its past, too. In 1921 one of the biggest race riots took place in Tulsa. At that time the Brady was the Tulsa Convention Hall. A large group of black residents were held at the hall–supposedly for their own safety. That's not how it worked out. Tragically, several black men were separated from the group and beaten to death in the "colored" men's restroom. The race riots are long over, but the spirits of those men remain behind, leaving the room icy cold. These days it is used for chair storage and employees still report being chilled to the bone when they step inside.

Address: **Brady Theater**
              105 W. Brady St.
              Tulsa, OK 74103-1818

Phone: (918) 582-2353

Tickets: Call the box office at (918) 582-7239

Directions: From I-44 heading southwest, exit on North Cheyenne Avenue. Travel south to West Brady. Turn left.

GILCREASE MUSEUM

The Gilcrease Museum was founded in 1949 to house the private collection of Thomas Gilcrease. When he died in 1962 he left his collection and his home and its surrounding acreage to the city of Tulsa. The original building was designed in the style of an Indian log house and has been expanded to a three-story structure. Here you'll see one of the most extensive collections of American art and artifacts, 23 acres of historic theme gardens, and maybe even the spirit of the museum's founder!

Thomas Gilcrease was born in 1890 in Louisiana. His family moved to the Tulsa area, which was then Indian Territory, to take advantage of his mother's rights as a Creek Indian. Gilcrease made some of his money from oil and attained even more through his marriage to his first wife. They had two children before they divorced. He later married Miss America of 1926. Gilcrease was one-eighth Creek and very much involved in his Native American heritage, enough to have a traditional Creek wedding ceremony on his front lawn instead of a society wedding.

He had the position to do what he wanted. He had the funds to purchase the art he loved. He had the generosity to leave it to the city for all the world to enjoy. It even appears that after death, he wants to remain as head curator.

Gilcrease's spirit has been seen in both the museum and in

Gilcrease Museum

his former home, now the home of the historical society. Anne Morand, a curator at the museum, crossed paths with Mr. Gilcrease after only a few weeks on the job. The senior curator had been showing her around the museum, the grounds and outbuildings. At that time the Gilcrease house was used for storage. As he wanted her to have the opportunity to look around undisturbed, and since visitors were wandering through the grounds, he locked the door to the house so the visitors wouldn't try to enter and then returned to his own office.

Anne spent a pleasant half hour looking at the various art objects stored in the house. During that time she heard footsteps overhead and the occasional creak of a floorboard. When she saw a man dressed in khaki clothes, a slouch hat, and wire-rimmed glasses come down the stairs, she simply assumed he worked there, perhaps as the gardener. She greeted him and he touched his hat in response and kept walking. Hearing the door open and close, she assumed he left. The senior curator came back for her later and Anne mentioned the man she had assumed was the gardener. She was surprised that he seemed upset, until he explained that it couldn't have been the gardener since the door had remained locked and the gardener had no key. The only other door was bolted.

He took Anne to a window and pointed out the gardener. It wasn't the man she had seen. At his request she provided a description. Upon hearing it, he went off to get a book and showed her a photo from it. She recognized the man immediately as the one she'd seen walking down the stairs. She thought it was a joke when he said it was Thomas Gilcrease, who had died years ago. But the book confirmed the identity of the man in the photo and she knew what she had seen. Although logic told her it was impossible, it had to be Thomas Gilcrease walking though his old home.

Anne has never seen Gilcrease's spirit again and, after speaking to others who had seen him, she learned that they had the experience only once as well. She also found that the others had no idea who he was when they'd seen him. There was nothing "ghostly" about Gilcrease's spirit. He looked just like anyone else. It was only later that they learned they'd actually seen a ghost.

So why is a man like Thomas Gilcrease, who managed to attain his life's dreams, not eager to attain his final reward? Anne wonders if this might not be his final reward, and presents an intriguing concept: "I am just optimistic enough," she says, "to hope that our time on earth might be prolonged, in whatever way, if we can remain to enjoy the things we loved."

Address:	**Gilcrease Museum**
	1400 Gilcrease Museum Road
	Tulsa, OK 74127
Phone:	(918) 596-2700
Hours:	Tuesday–Saturday, 9:00 am to 5:00 pm
	Sundays and holidays: 11:00 am to 5:00 pm
	(except Christmas)
	Open Mondays from Memorial Day to Labor Day
	Admission: Suggested donation $3 adults, $5 family

Directions: From I-44 heading southwest from Tulsa, exit on North Union Avenue traveling south. Turn right on Charles Page Boulevard. Bear right on Riverside Drive. Take the next left to North Gilcrease Museum Road.

CONSTANTINE
THEATER

Pawhuska, Oklahoma ———————————

The Constantine Theater is part of the historic downtown district of Pawhuska. It began as a hotel in the 1870s and generally served "drummers" (the traveling salesmen of those days) and the Osage Indians who came into town on business. C.A. Constantine, a Greek immigrant, purchased the hotel and in 1914 opened it as a theater for live vaudeville performances. Constantine sold the building in 1927 and it was converted into a movie theater. It closed down in the 1960s and essentially stayed that way, as so many buildings do in downtown areas, until the Pawhuska Downtown Revitalization and Preservation Association acted in 1985. The Constantine Theater was one of the buildings earmarked for restoration and is now called the Constantine Center.

Janet Holcombe was instrumental in organizing the effort and she was also one of the first people to wonder just what was going on in the Constantine Theater. She frequently worked in the building by herself and took care to lock the doors, but often heard footsteps, though she knew no one was around and sometimes felt a presence. Once, while working in the foyer, she heard the sound of hard wooden heels walk across the stage.

Soon people became nervous about working in the building. Stories of a ghost began to escalate and any strange thing that happened was blamed on the ghost. At one point, all the wiring in the building had been removed yet one light remained

Constantine Theater

on, sometimes flickering. Everyone was certain the ghost had something to do with it until it was discovered that the light was wired to the Old Constantine Confectionery Store in the adjoining building. Since this also belonged to Constantine, he was able to move from one business to the other without fumbling for a light.

Today the stories have calmed down, but even now that the theater is restored and operating, the strange activity continues. "We all agree the spirit is active," says Eileen Monger, referring to the volunteer theater group. "You hear footsteps and strange sounds you can't identify. You can lock the doors at night and find them open later." Even the alarm system has gone off when no one is in the building. One experience in particular stands out in Eileen's mind.

She'd been giving a slide presentation for a group and knew she'd be repeating the same presentation in a few days. She left everything set up and locked the door. The building was closed. No one was inside until she returned. When she did, she began her presentation and found one slide turned upside down. Hardly a frightening experience, just a hint to let her know that the ghost wanted some attention.

Once they entertained the thought that they might have a ghost, the next question was who is it? Most of the theater group call her Aunt Sassy, after one of Constantine's daughters, Sappho. This is where Janet Holcombe disagrees. Sappho was very petite and the footsteps are much too heavy for her. She believes the ghost is a man. Could it be Constantine, watching over his theater, or his daughter? You may have to come and decide for yourself.

Address: **Constantine Theater**
                 110 W. Main
                 Pawhuska, OK 74056

Phone: For performance information contact the
                 Chamber of Commerce at (918) 287-1208

Directions: Highway 60 goes through the middle of downtown Pawhuska. The Constantine Center is on the south side of the street.

SPIRO MOUNDS

Spiro Mounds is a place of great mystery. Consisting of twelve earthen mounds, it was a site of important religious ceremony for the people who lived in the surrounding area from 700 to 1450 A.D. The area was abandoned at that time though no one knows why. Today the mounds are a protected archeological site, a source of spiritual energy, and a source of some amazing stories.

Reports of blue lights flashing over the burial mound go back as far as 1900, but it's quite possible the lights were flashing long before that. The depression years brought people to the area who were desperate for anything they could sell and once the mounds were disturbed by these commercial diggers, things got very strange around Spiro. The diggers who came in the early thirties, looted the mounds looking for pots and other artifacts. They dug up bodies in search of precious metals and stones and blasted the entrance to one of the burial chambers to cover up their work.

The Oklahoma Antiquities law was enacted to put an end to such desecration and appointed the University of Oklahoma to regulate commercial digging, though it did not stop all the diggers. Some landowners in the area allowed them back on their lands. The diggers didn't get away with it for long, however. What the law couldn't stop, the curse did.

People who live and work in the area are familiar with what are called the "curse stories." In 1936 one of the diggers was reported missing. His body was found and an autopsy indicated that he had drowned. The strange part was that he'd been found in a dry river bed that had not held any water for over a month. Another digger was driving down Highway 59 when his brakes went out. He hit a tree with such force the engine was shoved back into the bed of the truck. When police examined the vehicle, they found the damage to the brakes looked as if they had been forced apart. Another site simply collapsed, burying a third digger.

All of this activity happened in the late thirties. No new deaths have been associated with Spiro Mounds or the curse. Today the spiritual activity is much more benign. Every winter a strange occurrence takes place at the visitors' center, usually in late December or January. The back door will open and you can hear footsteps and creaking from above as if someone were walking across the roof. Then the front door will open. An hour or so later the process is reversed. Visitors have also said they've felt a presence at the site. Some even say they believe someone is trying to speak to them. This kind of activity may be strange, but it's a lot easier to take than the curse deaths.

Address:	**Spiro Mounds Interpretive Center** Route 2, Box 339AA Spiro, OK 74959
Phone:	(918) 962-2062
Hours:	5/1–9/30, 9 am–7 pm Monday- Saturday, Sunday 1 pm–7 pm 10/1–4/30, 9 am–5 pm Monday-Saturday Sunday 1 pm–5 pm

Directions: Spiro Mounds State Park is in northeastern LeFlore County, 10 miles west of the Oklahoma-Arkansas state line. Exit I-40 at US 59 South. Travel 16 miles to Highway 9. Turn east to the Mayo Lock and Dam Road.

STONE LION INN

What could be a better setting for a murder mystery than a haunted mansion? Okay, so no one was murdered here–at least not that we know of–but Becky Luker, owner of the Stone Lion Inn since 1986, does host murder mystery parties. While the murders may be staged, the ghosts appear to be quite real.

One of Guthrie's historic homes, the Stone Lion Inn dates back to 1907 when the Houghton family outgrew their previous house right next door and moved into this spacious and elegant mansion. They suffered a tragedy when one of their twelve children died. Augusta, only eight years old, contracted whooping cough, and it is suspected that she died from an overdose of the cough syrup of the day, which was heavily laced with opium and codeine. It is her ghost that is believed to be haunting the mansion today.

Not long after moving into the Houghton Mansion, the Luker family would find their youngest son's toys scattered about one of the third floor rooms. He kept his toys in a large closet up there and knowing he'd put them away, he blamed his brother for scattering them about. The brother denied the charges, but as the days passed, it became clear that someone was getting the toys out at night and playing with them. They were put away every evening and found all over the room the next morning. When Becky finally put a lock on the closet door, she expected an end to the problem, but she was wrong. The situation continued and they knew something very strange was going on, and not only with the toys. They also heard little footsteps on the third floor at night and a door open and close.

Stone Lion Inn

It wasn't long before they had a visit from the remaining members of the Houghton family and learned about Augusta. The family explained that they had kept their toys in the same closet and often snuck upstairs late at night to play after their parents were asleep. This usually took place between ten and midnight, the same time the Lukers heard the footsteps. It seems that Augusta is still playing. One time she broke from her usual schedule and tried to get in the closet while eight-year-old Ral Luker was still in the room. He heard her and ran.

There is another side to Augusta that is not quite so carefree. Several guests have reported being awakened in the morning by a pat on the cheek. When they opened their eyes, no one was there, but they all had the impression of a small child who seemed lost and looking for her mother.

Augusta is not the Stone Lion Inn's only ghost. During the 1920s the house was a funeral home and later a boarding house. Either might be the source of the ghost who ignores the no smoking policy. Not only can you smell the acrid cigars, you can see the curls of smoke hanging on the air. The maids have claimed to see him, hiding behind the heating system, wearing a dark suit and top hat.

There have been two reports where a ghost has been quite helpful. On one occasion a guest was unable to turn off the light in her ceiling fan and decided to go ahead and sleep with it on. Just as she settled into bed, she felt someone climb up on the bed and turn off the light. Another incident happened to Ral when he was a child. He was tired and lay down on his mother's bed to watch television. He felt someone climb in beside him and begin rubbing his back. When he turned, no one was there, but he could feel someone breathing.

While not always performing good deeds, the family accepts the ghosts, the footsteps, the closing doors, flickering lights and occasional laughter. The guests love it.

Address: **Stone Lion Inn**
                1016 W. Warner
                Guthrie, OK 73044

Phone: (405) 282-0012

Directions: Guthrie is 25 miles north of Oklahoma City. From I-35, take Exit 157 west to Guthrie. Turn left at Highway 33 (or Noble). Turn right on 10th. The first cross street is Warner. Turn left.

GRAY BROTHERS BUILDING

The Gray Brothers Building has stood sentry over its corner of Oklahoma Street since 1890. It began as a grocery, expanded to a feed store, then became a bank and several retail establishments. It is one of more than two thousand historic buildings in Guthrie, Oklahoma, but it is the only one where Ivan Ridge chose to spend his afterlife.

Since the 1930s, Ivan owned the barber shop located in the basement of this building and lived with his mail-order bride on the second floor.

David Denton, the owner of a coffee shop named The Red Earth Mud opened his business in 1995. The store needed renovation and that's when he first ran into Ivan. He was working with a friend uncovering the stained-glass windows in the face of the building. His friend was outside on a ladder. David was on scaffolding inside—alone, which made it all the more surprising when he smelled cigar smoke. The scent was so strong it was as if it had been blown into his face.

That was the beginning. He'd hear sounds of moving in the room above the shop, something being dragged across the floor. Machines were turned off when they were on, and on when they were off, and the music from the radio would get louder and louder, although no one had turned it up.

Then, a psychic friend of David's sister dropped by for a visit. She told him he had a ghost. She described the ghost as

The Gray Brothers Building

a big man with a mustache and red suspenders. She saw him as dirty and that his first name was Ivan and his last was the name of some bridge. David, not certain he believed this, reported the news to the other business owners who shared the building. He told Laurah Kilbourn, who's shop, Extra Special Fabric and Custom Sewing, is located in the basement. From the look of shock on her face he could see that the description fit someone she knew. She was certain it was Ivan Ridge, whose barber shop used to be located right in the space she now occupies.

Laurah had known Ivan in his life. He'd died in 1982 and was quite a character in the small town. The "big man" part of the psychic's description was no exaggeration. Ivan was too big to fit in a car, so he drove a motorcycle with a side car, which drew enough attention that the neighborhood children teased him without mercy. If that wasn't enough, he was covered with tattoos (which might explain why the psychic saw him as dirty), and had a mail-order bride.

Other business owners in the building had also experienced the ghost's tricks. At Our Corner, the furniture store next door, owners Patti Davis and Carolyn Blevins have also smelled Ivan's cigars. They've heard their music boxes play when no one has touched them, not just a note or two of music either, the boxes would play "a good little lick," as Patti would say. They have heard banging on their pipes, and once heard the windchimes tinkling although they remained undisturbed. Once the bottle in their water cooler was mysteriously changed while the building was locked up for the night. A photo taken in the shop revealed an indistinguishable face when developed that wasn't there when the camera clicked. If that was Ivan, it was the only time he's shown himself.

Downstairs, Laurah Kilbourn has an electric eye that buzzes when someone enters her shop through the front door. It does some suspicious buzzing when no one is around. Clothes have been pulled off racks and displays have been altered—also when the store has been closed for the night.

Ivan seems to be enjoying his time as a spirit. The merchants at the Gray Brothers Building are congenial company and he keeps himself amused by playing tricks on them. He does as he pleases, though he usually complies when they ask him to settle down. As far as they are concerned, Ivan is welcome to stick around as long as he likes. Maybe you'd like to stop in and have a cup of coffee with him?

Address:	**Gray Brothers Building** 101 W. Oklahoma Ave. Guthrie, OK 73044
Phone:	(405) 282-1144

Directions: Guthrie is 25 miles north of Oklahoma City. From I-35, take Exit 157 west; turn left on Highway 33 (or Noble) to Division St. Turn left on Division to Oklahoma Avenue (2 blocks south.)

OVERHOLSER MANSION

Oklahoma City, Oklahoma — — — — — — — — —

The Overholser Mansion is a beautifully-preserved slice of Oklahoma history. The Gothic home was completed in 1903 by Henry Overholser and remained in the family until 1972 when it was purchased by the Oklahoma City Historical Society. You can tour the mansion or stop by for a few ghost stories during one of their storytelling sessions. You might even walk away with a story of your own if you happen to see the spirit of Anna Overholser.

The Overholsers were a prominent family in Oklahoma City. Henry Overholser was a mover and shaker who built the city's first waterworks, theater, and street car line, among his other contributions to the city's growth. His second wife, Anna, was a cultural and social leader who did a great deal of entertaining in their home. They were a happy family who seemed to enjoy their lives. Maybe that's why Anna's spirit lingers in the mansion.

Site Administrator, Bill Fullhart, would prefer the mansion be known for its historic value, but he is willing to share what he knows of the Overholser spirits. The first experience he'd heard of was prior to the historical society's purchase of the home. A cook working in the kitchen saw a door close by itself. Either that was all it took, or that was the last straw, because then and there she "put on her bonnet and left."

Once volunteers from the historical society began work on

restoring and preserving the home, reports of strange occurrences flourished. One group of about six people working in the upper bedrooms decided to break for lunch, but before leaving, one of them smoothed out the folds in a bedspread. When they returned, the spread was mussed, as if someone had been lying on it. The spread and the majority of articles in the house are all original and handled with great care. No one in the group would have been so rough with the spread, and no one was in the house while they were gone. On other occasions, a group of volunteers has opened the house in the morning to find a curtain pulled back as if someone had been looking out the window at the street below.

The spirit of Anna Overholser has also been seen in the mansion from time to time. Bill Fullhart remembers a visit his grandson made to the mansion. While in the hall, the boy was startled by something. When Fullhart questioned him, the frightened boy replied that "something without legs just walked in front of me." Further questions drew out the information that it had been a woman with something piled on her head and something around her neck. Fullhart had been distracted and had not seen the apparition himself, and while he had heard about the ghost, he knew his grandson hadn't. He had no reason to believe the boy was making up a story. He showed the boy a picture of Anna Overholser, with her hair piled up on her head, wearing a high-collared Worth gown. The boy recognized her immediately as the apparition he'd seen. Others have seen the spirit cross from the library to the music room, where she had entertained her guests.

If you tour the mansion, you're not likely to hear any talk of ghosts. But if it's a ghost story you're after, drop in on one of the Overholser's storytelling events. You'll hear stories from the mansion as well as other Oklahoma haunts and folklore.

Address:	Overholser Mansion
	405 NW 15th Street
	Oklahoma City, OK 73103
Phone:	(405) 528-8485
	Please call for information on tours and storytelling.

Directions: From I-44, take I-235 south for 3.5 miles to NW 15th Street.

ARAPAHO CEMETERY

North of Clinton, is the tiny town of Arapaho. Quiet and peaceful, this is not a place you might associate with a ghost. But if you travel just north of town, you'll find Arapaho Cemetery, where one spirit is reported to haunt the grave of another. If you happen to be standing near the center of this small cemetery, you may hear the mournful voice of George Smith crying for his daughter Robina. Nineteen-year-old Robina Smith died in a car accident in 1936 on US Highway 183. This was certainly tragedy enough for her father, but what troubled him even more deeply was that he believed Robina's soul would not find salvation because she had never accepted the Lord.

Robina's Headstone

George Smith still mourns his daughter's death even after his own. After he died in 1972, reports of the voice at Robina's grave began. George Smith's cry has been described as beginning with a deep moan. Then a masculine voice cries out "Oh, no! Oh, my God! Robina has not been saved!" Among the many reports is one from a minister who heard the voice during a graveside funeral service. Another came from a geologist who was trying to find a scientific explanation for the sound. To the best of our knowledge, he was unsuccessful.

Directions: From I-40 exit US Highway 183 in Clinton. Travel north about 6 miles and watch for an unmarked road on the east side of the highway. The cemetery is about half a mile down that road on the right.

THE NAT

At the edge of a mile-long, trendy antique district sits a strange, almost castle-like building simply called, "the Nat." Shortened from natatorium, an old-fashion term for an indoor swimming pool, the structure was built in 1922. The pool, one of only three in the country at the time, was covered in 1923 so it could be utilized year round.

Three years later, J. D. Tucker purchased the building. The enterprising new owner made some big changes. He put a floor over the swimming pool and converted the building into a ballroom, calling it the Nat Dine & Dance Palace.

During the crash of 1929, when money became scarce, the Nat used different promotions to entice guests to come to the nightclub. New cars furnished by local dealers, Navajo blankets, Chinese slippers, records, cash in balloons and even hosiery (a highly sought item during that period) were given away to boost attendance.

The Nat Cafe was added to the north elevation in 1935, providing an entrance for its patrons driving on Route 66. The fortress-like facade was a prime example of some of the whimsical roadway architecture that was so popular in the thirties.

From the twenties through the forties, customers were entertained by the big band sound. The Dorsey Brothers, Duke Ellington and Guy Lombardo were just a few of the big bands that performed at this popular nightspot. When the "rock era" hit the nation, a younger crowd was drawn in to hear Little Richard, Buddy Holly and the Crickets, and Roy Orbison.

The Nat

Soon after purchasing the Nat, Mike Baker, one of the owners, noticed he was chilled every time he went upstairs. It didn't take long before he realized he was never alone in the newly-remodeled antique store. Not only was he hearing strange noises, but when he'd arrive at work in the morning he'd find that someone had rearranged the furniture during the night–while the building was locked.

Bubbles, a psychic, is a member of a band that performs at the Nat. She claims that the upstairs area, where the dining room and lounge were located, has quite a bit of supernatural activity. Gambling used to take place on this floor, which may be why some of the spirits are reluctant to leave. This is also where Bubbles first encountered a female apparition. The ghost wears a white dress with a red stain on the bodice. Bubbles learned that this woman spent many a rowdy evening gambling upstairs with some of the town's most prominent citizens. On one occasion, one of them poured a glass of red wine down her dress.

The ballroom floor is quite popular with the various ghosts, as well. When the band performs, Bubbles can see couples gliding on the dance floor. In October of 1996, the Nat had an all night ghost hunt, setting up tape recorders and video cameras. The cameras kept shutting off, but the sponsors were successful in getting an audio recording of a woman singing and a drum solo playing in the background.

Bubbles has also seen several ghosts of children. She was perplexed as to why they would be hanging around what used to be a dance palace, but then she learned that a previous owner had allowed kids to rollerskate on the ballroom floor after school.

With all the spirits at the Nat, there is only one area where the psychic and the owners all feel a sense of evil. This is a room towards the back of the store. During the days of the Nat Dine & Dance Palace, this was the coat check room. It was here that an employee was viciously raped long ago.

If you don't mind climbing down a ladder to the basement, Mike will show you an unusual painting. A beautiful young woman, with bobbed hair, dressed in 1920s clothing, was painted right on the wall. But be extra careful climbing down. Mike and ladders don't seem to go together. While he was using a ladder in a storage room, it began to shake uncontrollably. Mike climbed off and released it, but it continued wobbling.

When you leave the Nat, be sure to observe the outside of the building. "Monty McGee and his Orchestra" was painted on the walls in 1942 but every time it's painted over, the words bleed through–another reminder that these spirits don't want to be forgotten.

Address:	**The Nat** 2705 W. 6th Street Amarillo, TX 79106
Phone:	(806) 371-8685
Hours:	Monday-Saturday 10:00 am-5:30 pm Sunday 1:00 pm-5:00 pm

Directions: From I-40, take the Georgia St. exit. Go north on Georgia to 6th Street (about 8 blocks). Turn left and continue to the Nat.

New Mexico

❶ **Tucumcari:** *Blue Moon Restaurant*
❷ **Madrid:** *Mine Shaft Tavern*
❸ **Santa Fe:**
      La Posada
      La Fonda Hotel
❹ **Algodones:** *Hacienda Vargas*
❺ **Bernalillo:** *La Hacienda Grande*
❻ **Corrales:** *Rancho de Corrales*
❼ **Los Lunas:** *Luna Mansion Restaurant*
❽ **Albuquerque:**
      Maria Teresa Restaurant
      KiMo Theater
      W. J. Marsh House
      Church Street Cafe

BLUE MOON RESTAURANT

The Sands-Dorsey Building, built at the turn of the century, has served this small community in many different aspects. Through the years people have opened up savings accounts, had prescriptions filled, picked up fine cigars and have enjoyed old-fashioned malts at Tucumcari's most unique building.

The Sands-Dorsey Building looks much like it did in the early 1900s. The Victorian pressed tin ceilings are 14 feet high and the terrazzo floor looks as it did in 1935 when it and the interior were redone in a sleek Art Deco design.

In the 1920s, the Commonwealth Bank shared the building with a dry goods store and pharmacy. When the bank folded during the Depression, Sands-Dorsey's Drug Company took over.

Even in small towns there are bits and pieces of scandal to keep tongues wagging. There is talk of booze stored in the basement of the building during Prohibition and hints of slot machines kept in the back hall well into the 1970s.

At one time the upstairs floor was used as a doctor's office, a lawyer's office, a dentist's office and a beauty shop. In 1981 the previous owners converted the second floor into living quarters.

The Big Dipper Cafe and Ice Cream Parlor opened up in 1995 after Charlene and Lee Miller purchased the building.

Blue Moon Restaurant and The Big Dipper Ice Cream Parlor

They have since renamed their cafe the Blue Moon Restaurant.

When Lee goes to one of the four basements, he always feels uncomfortable. "I feel I'm not alone, even though I'm the only one down there. It's always chilly, an eerie-feeling chilly." A spirit looking for the booze?

The basement is broken down to four separate rooms and surprisingly the more modern of the four is the room that Lee's dogs refuse to enter. No amount of coaxing can convince the animals to accompany their owner when he is in that room. Cabinets and cases built years before line the walls. Are the dogs aware of some supernatural entities due to their sensitivity?

They have a most unusual ghost that likes to play tricks with the Tucumcari Police Department. It has to be storming out when the spirit gets into the mood to place 911 calls. When an officer answers he always finds a dead line. Charlene and Lee know for a fact that no one in the building could have placed those calls. This has occurred several times and so far, neither the Millers nor the Tucumcari Police Department can explain how this can humanly happen.

Don't let the spirits that roam this old building keep you from enjoying some ice cream at The Big Dipper Cafe or a great meal at the Blue Moon Restaurant. Expect to be questioned by the police, however, if you happen to be there when the wind begins to blow and torrents of rain start to come down.

Address: **Blue Moon Restautrant**
Tucumcari, NM 88401

Phone: (505) 461-4430

Hours: Monday - Saturday 9:00 am to sunset
Closed Sundays

Directions: Take Exit 332 from I-40. This is 1st Street. Go north to the second traffic light (Main St.). Go west on Main Street 1 block to the corner of Main and Second Streets.

Note: Tucumcari Boulevard is the old Route 66. In 1948, Route 66 was moved north to Main Street.

MINE SHAFT TAVERN

The area around Madrid, just 26 miles south of La Cienaga, is the oldest coal mining region in New Mexico, with evidence suggesting that the mineral was mined as early as the late 1850s. Because Madrid was one of only a few places in the world where both hard and soft coal were found, it became a flourishing mining town. Oxen hauled hard coal from Madrid all the way to St. Louis. At its peak in the 1920s and thirties the population reached 2,500. During World War II the Madrid Mines provided Los Alamos, New Mexico with 20,000 tons of coal, enabling them to build the first atomic bomb.

Production started to dwindle when the switch to natural gas and diesel fuel slowly cut out the need for coal. Doom came in 1959 when Los Alamos, Madrid's last major customer for coal, made the switch to gas. Almost overnight Madrid became a ghost town. Only a few hardy souls remained, reluctant to leave a lifetime of memories.

The 1970s was the time of the counter culture with artists and hippies purchasing the miners' shacks at bargain basement prices. They renovated homes and opened shops to sell their wares. Slowly Madrid came back to life.

Today, the town with the majestic Ortiz mountains for a background, boasts a population of 400. This quaint mountain community, with its shops, galleries and restaurants, has become a popular stop along The Turquoise Trail.

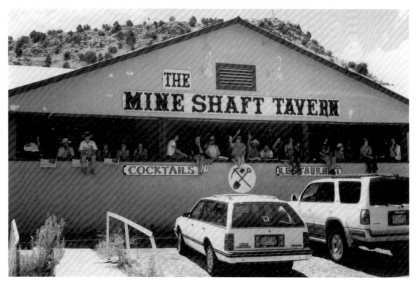

Mine Shaft Tavern

To get a real feel of the history of this colorful town, visit the Mine Shaft Tavern. It opened for business in 1946 and it was here the miners gathered for farewell drinks on that fateful day when they received the news that the mines were closing.

The Mine Shaft Tavern, purchased from the Albuquerque and Cerrillos Coal Company and restored in 1982, may no longer be an oasis for the miners who worked in Madrid, but it's certainly one of the last great roadhouses in America. The tavern's 40-foot lodge-pole pine bar is the longest stand-up bar in New Mexico. Behind the bar a long narrow room was designed to resemble the interior of a coal mine tunnel.

Like so many mining towns, Madrid had its share of tragedies. At one time one of the mines collapsed and several people were killed. The Mine Shaft Tavern has had enough paranormal experiences to convince anyone that some of the old miners are still hanging around, enjoying their favorite watering hole.

Bartenders, as well as guests, have seen glasses fall on their own and break; doors that open and swing back and forth; sounds that can be heard coming from six-inch adobe walls; and after closing hours, objects that are mysteriously moved about. Perhaps the most unsettling occurrence is when employees look in a mirror and instead of seeing their own reflections, they see that of a ghost!

After sundown the darkness of this living ghost town, in the middle of nowhere, is eerie. With only the stars providing light, it is the perfect setting where the dead haunt the living. And, if you're really quiet, you may be able to hear sounds of a long-deceased Indian who roams the ballpark area at the north end of town.

Address: **Mine Shaft Tavern**
2946 State Highway 14
Madrid, NM 87010

Phone: (505) 473-0743

Hours: Daily 11:00 am - 11:00 pm

Directions: From I-40 exit east of Albuquerque, travel northeast on State Highway 14 (The Turquoise Trail), toward Santa Fe. From Santa Fe, travel west to State Highway 14 and then southwest toward Albuquerque. Madrid is two-thirds of the way to Santa Fe from Albuquerque.

LA POSADA

The La Posada was originally built in 1882 by Abraham Stabb for his wife Julie. The three-story Victorian home was Santa Fe's first brick building, but at the beginning of the century fire destroyed the third floor. The ballroom, which had been on that floor, was used by Julie and Abraham for entertaining and dancing. The Stabbs were known for their lavish parties with prominent guests always in attendance.

Julie and Abraham had a large family of seven children. Their seventh child died shortly after birth and Mrs. Stabb's hair turned grey overnight. She became so despondent that she confined herself to her bedroom until her death in 1896 at the age of 52.

Room 256, which had been Julie's bedroom, is just one place where unexplained occurrences have taken place. A couple awoke in the middle of the night when they heard water running in their bathtub. Although both faucets were turned off, water continued rushing out of the valves. They checked out immediately.

In the winter of 1993, guests staying in the same room asked for more blankets. After sleeping for several hours, they woke up shivering, only to find all of the blankets had been thrown in the corner of the room. They packed and left before daylight.

A chimney sweeper working outside happened to glance toward Room 256 and saw a woman peering through the window, although the room was unoccupied. He claimed she

Portrait of Julie Stabb, the spirit of La Posada

looked just like the woman in a portrait he had seen in the drawing room; the painting was of Julie.

Mrs. Stabb can be mischievous; she especially likes to play games with the key to her bedroom. When the authors of this book were given a tour of the hotel, the key to open the door simply would not work. Another key was tried and, after much difficulty, we were finally able to get a glimpse of where Julie spent her final days.

She does venture to other areas of the house, although she is never seen on the lavish grounds. An employee working in the hotel's bar early one morning, getting it ready to open, spotted Julie, dressed in white lace, sitting in a chair. A few minutes later the employee glanced up, but Julie's spirit had already disappeared.

Several people have seen Julie, dressed in black, ascending the grand staircase while others just feel her presence. One young clerk explained her experience, " I walked into a cold spot and it felt like I had walked right through her spirit."

Julie has shown no inclination to leave her former home. Of course, as elegant as La Posada is, who can blame her?

Address:	**La Posada**
	330 E. Palace Avenue
	Santa Fe, NM 87501
Phone:	(800) 727-5276
	(505) 986-0000

Directions: From I-25, take St. Francis exit and follow St. Francis Drive north. Turn right on Paseo de Peralta–state Hwy. 589 (you will circle the downtown area) to Palace Avenue. La Posada will be on your right at that intersection.

La Posada

Photo courtesy Noel Bonnin

LA FONDA HOTEL

"The Inn at the End of the Santa Fe Trail" means just that. The original adobe hotel occupied the corner of the Santa Fe Trail and San Francisco Street, where the trail ends at the town's central plaza. Since 1610, there has been an inn or "fonda" at this site to accommodate travelers.

The history of La Fonda is as interesting as the ghosts that roam this old historic adobe building. Through the centuries the hotel had been the destination of trappers, traders, merchants, politicians and all others who made their way along the Santa Fe trail. After the 1828 discovery of gold in the mountains south of town, the hotel's business prospered as well as its saloon and casino.

In 1884 the inn was purchased by an American couple who changed its name to the U. S. Hotel. Like so many other establishments in that period of time, the U. S. Hotel had its share of violence. One guest lost his life when a lynch mob hung the patron in the hotel's back yard in 1857. In 1867 the Honorable John P. Slough, Chief Justice of the Territorial Supreme Court, was shot to death in the hotel lobby.

The hotel was once again sold and renamed The Exchange Hotel, a name it would keep for the next 60 years. When Mrs. D. B. Davis, the last great hostess of The Exchange, gave up her lease, the once elaborate hotel began to deteriorate. The Exchange struggled and became a boarding house in 1907, before being demolished in 1919.

In 1920, investors bought stock to finance the present-day

La Plazuela Restaurant at La Fonda

La Fonda, building the hotel on the same site, the southeast corner of the plaza. In 1925 the Atchison, Topeka & Santa Fe Railroad rescued the hotel when that business venture failed. The railroad then leased it to Fred Harvey. From 1926 to 1969, La Fonda was one of the Harvey Houses, a renowned chain of fine hotels.

Today, La Fonda's Spanish pueblo architecture blends in with Santa Fe's rich cultural heritage. Situated in the foothills of the Sangre de Cristo Mountains, the Southwestern hotel has attracted celebrities from Kit Carson to John F. Kennedy to Doc Severinson.

Guests dining in the enclosed sky-lit courtyard restaurant may experience more than a good meal. More than 100 years ago, a man who gambled away his company's money committed suicide by jumping down a well. The well was located outside The Exchange. The La Plazuela restaurant was built directly over the well and more than a few people have seen a man walk to the center of the room and jump, as if into an unseen hole, and then vanish.

Another ghost, a female, would appear on the second floor until the new ballroom was built in the 1990s. Speculation is that it's the spirit of a bride who, spending her wedding night at the hotel in the 1920s, was murdered by her former boyfriend.

Other reports of paranormal activity include sounds of children playing in the hallway, as well as babies crying, and doors that open and shut on their own. Diners have described a woman dressed in red walking by their table saying, "help me, help me." One employee reported that something was breathing down his neck while he was in the lounge.

A variety of ghosts to be sure, but they all have one thing in common–they're in no hurry to leave "The Inn at the End of the Santa Fe Trail."

Address:	**La Fonda Hotel**
	100 East San Francisco Street
	Santa Fe, NM 87501
Phone:	(800) 523-5002
	(505) 982-5511

Directions: From I-25 exit Old Pecos Trail. Turn left and proceed north to the third traffic light. Turn right and follow Old Pecos Trail into town. This street will merge into Old Santa Fe Trail. Continue on Old Santa Fe Trail until you reach San Francisco Street. La Fonda Hotel will be on your right. Turn right (away from the plaza and toward the cathedral) and proceed to the La Fonda garage at the end of the hotel on the right.

HACIENDA VARGAS BED & BREAKFAST

If you think you might like a spiritual experience but you don't want to deal with a lot of ghostly pranks, you might find the perfect place in Hacienda Vargas. Paul Vargas, owner of this bed and breakfast, definitely prefers the former and he ought to know the difference. He and his family spent two years living with very active spirits in a former home in California. He saw and heard things that he knew could not be real, his imagination or a dream.

The spirits of the Hacienda Vargas Bed and Breakfast are not quite like that. They are much more subtle and much easier to take. They simply permeate this old adobe dwelling with a sense of goodwill, an ease or comfort that is undoubtedly spiritual, as if the building had absorbed the spirits of its former owners. Paul noticed it from the first time he walked in. The feeling was so strong it made him do something unusual for him. He bought the place on impulse in 1991 and spent nine months renovating it.

Hacienda Vargas is situated on historic El Camino Real, a route founded in the 16th century that has lasted into modern times as a portion of Route 66. The building was once a stagecoach stop, a post office and a private home owned by the Vigil family. There is no tragedy associated with this dwelling, only happiness, peace and tranquility, which might explain

Hacienda Vargas

why Hacienda Vargas stirs those feelings today. Guests consistently comment on experiencing a sense of tranquility while staying there, and while Paul is unaware of any specific ghosts, a psychic saw a spirit she believed was the grandmother of the Vigil family walking through the courtyard.

So what provides this spiritual feeling? Is it the ghost, the house itself or just the magic of New Mexico? Paul Vargas doesn't know for sure but he and his guests can't deny the existence of something spiritual here.

Address: **Hacienda Vargas Bed & Breakfast**
P.O. Box 307
Algodones, NM 87001

Phone: (505) 867-9115

Directions: From I-25 take Exit 248 West to Highway 313 (El Camino Real). Turn south. Hacienda Vargas is on the right.

LA HACIENDA GRANDE BED & BREAKFAST

If you happen to buy a haunted dwelling, do you have to put up with the ghost's antics, pranks, and just plain bad manners? Not according to Shoshana Zimmerman. Shoshana, along with her brother, Daniel Buop, opened La Hacienda Grande as a bed and breakfast in 1993.

Located in Bernalillo, this 250-year-old building sits on land of even older history. In the 1540s, Coronado used this site for two years as his home base while he explored New Mexico and wiped out local Indian tribes until he finally moved on to other territory. Long before Coronado, this was sacred land to the Tuquex Pueblo tribe. Hacienda Grande itself was the center of the Spanish village that grew around Bernalillo and home to the Gallegos family in the 1700s. In the 1800s it became a stagecoach stop. With so much history you might think it was full of spirits. You'd be right.

Shoshana had been told that the inn had been built on sacred land. To appease the Tuquex spirits, they created a medicine wheel area outside the kitchen. She has had no problems with them, but the Spanish spirits are another story. They spent most of their time in the kitchen, which used to be the chapel, making mischief. These were very active and playful spirits. They would turn off the vent over the stove, causing smoke to fill the oven and, when the door

Spiritual energy can be felt near this tree in the Courtyard at La Hacienda Grande.

was opened, the kitchen. Shoshana decided to get help with her problem. She'd been told about a man who could communicate with spirits. He convinced the Spanish spirits to move out to the courtyard and leave their old chapel behind. To help make the transition, he had Shoshana place a religious statue in the courtyard. Shoshana has never had another problem in the kitchen. Since then though, there has been a strong energy around a tree in the center of the courtyard. If you place a hand near this spot you can feel a force or vibration.

The only spirit Shoshana has seen in the house appeared when she first moved in. After experiencing some sleeplessness, she began to feel it was due to the way her bed was placed. So, she turned the bed and stood in the area where the bed had been. That's when she saw the spirit, a small woman with her hair severely pulled back. The spirit gave the impression of anger and unhappiness, a very negative energy. With the help of some friends, Shoshana encouraged this woman to move on. She has never seen the spirit or felt her presence again.

There are some spirits that insist on sticking around no

An ancient spirit dwells on the roof of La Hacienda Grande.

matter what you do. Another ghost she calls Leroy makes his presence known with an odor. No one can quite describe this smell but those who work here have come into contact with it. When they do, his spirit must be very close, for if they simply turn their heads, the odor is gone. Shoshana has also invited Leroy to move on, but to no avail. He shows up less than he used to, but he still drops in from time to time–their noses let them know.

The last of Hacienda Grande's spirits is an Indian who occupies a corner of the roof. Shoshana has not seen him, but friends and guests have. They have also heard the sound of drums and dancing on the roof. Perhaps a long-gone spirit from the Tuquex Pueblo tribe is still protecting his land.

Address: **La Hacienda Grande Bed & Breakfast**
21 Baros Lane
Bernalillo, NM 87004

Phone: (505) 867-1887

Directions: From I-25 take Exit 242 west half of a mile to Camino del Pueblo North. Travel half a mile to Baros Lane. La Hacienda Grande is on the left at the end of the lane.

RANCHO de CORRALES RESTAURANT

Formerly known as the Territorial House, this ancient adobe hacienda was built in 1801 by Diego Montoya. Patrons visiting this exquisite restaurant feel that they're transported into the Spanish colonial era with the abundance of wrought iron and heavy carved doors.

Not only does the Rancho de Corrales provide fine meals in an elegant setting, they also provide the spirits–not the kind you drink. Although the employees have accepted the spirits, they try to avoid being in the building alone.

A glamorous high-society couple, murder and clandestine love affairs: the ingredients for a "movie of the week" or a Gothic novel! However, this weave of events actually happened to Mr. and Mrs. Luis Emberto, who purchased the property in 1883. Neither Luis nor his wife Louisa believed in keeping their marriage vows sacred and it ended up costing them their lives.

At one of their lavish dinner parties, their son killed a woman he thought was his father's mistress. Luis moved out of the house, believing his wife Louisa had encouraged the murder. Before leaving the hacienda, he threatened to kill her, as well as her lover.

In 1898 Mr. Emberto carried out his threat. Louisa knew why her husband had returned and ran for her gun, but she

Rancho de Corrales Restaurant

didn't move fast enough. He fired twice, killing her. An armed posse hunted him down and Luis was slaughtered in a lengthy gun battle.

Because of the scandalous circumstances surrounding their deaths, the Embertos were not allowed to be buried in a church cemetery. They were entombed on the property, and some believe their restless spirits come out at night.

In 1987 the Jaramillo, Romero and Torrez families purchased the restaurant. It wasn't long before the ghosts made their appearances. An employee was alone in the banquet room when he was astonished to witness chairs being stacked on top of each other with no visible help. On another occasion, while in the same room, he realized he wasn't alone when he saw the glowing red tip of a cigarette or cigar floating in the air.

The bar area is frequented by more than just mortals. The bartender, who has worked at the restaurant for more than ten years, reports that she has often had a female ghost wearing a long, white flowing gown, seat herself on a bar stool then melt away as she watched. She has observed this same spirit in other parts of the building too, and when she approaches, the spirit simply disappears.

One night after business hours, four employees were

unwinding after putting in a long day. Suddenly they heard a bottle fall into the trash can that sat next to their table. Because they were the only occupants in the room they would have known if one of them had tossed the bottle into the container. A spirit enjoying a drink or two with them?

The playful ghosts make certain that the staff as well as the customers know they're around. The owners always check the bathroom before locking up, but it is common for them to find the faucets running full blast the following morning. And it's not unusual for doors to open and close on their own or for customers to hear noises of unknown origins.

If you decide to have dinner at the Rancho de Corrales, take a few extra minutes to explore the grounds. The graves of Luis and Louisa Emberto lie across the irrigation ditch to the west of the restaurant. Remember, they're still roaming about, so don't be surprised if you encounter them!

Address:	**Rancho de Corrales Restaurant** 4895 Corrales Road Corrales, NM
Phone:	(505) 897-3131
Hours:	Tuesday-Friday 4:30 pm-9:00 pm Saturday 11:00 am-9:00 pm Sunday 10:00 am-9:00 pm Monday - closed

Directions: From Albuquerque, take I-25 north about 5 miles to the Alameda exit. Travel west on Alameda for 4 miles (crossing the Rio Grande). At the second traffic light (Corrales Road), turn right and travel 2.9 miles to the restaurant.

LUNA MANSION RESTAURANT

The Luna family, a powerful name in the political and social circles of the area, had a 35,000 acre ranch the Santa Fe Railroad wanted. In the late 1870s, the railroad offered to build them a new house in exchange for some of their property. Taking advantage of the proposal, the family had a mansion built in Southern colonial style architecture, although the basic construction was adobe.

The Luna Mansion, now a restaurant, is still the home of Josefita Manderfield Otero, one of the original owners. Although she passed away in 1912, she refuses to leave the home she loved so much.

Josefita's favorite place is the lounge on the second floor. This room had been her bedroom, so it's understandable that she'd be drawn to this part of the building. In 1993, the owner's three-year-old daughter was quietly watching television in the lounge. Suddenly she rushed downstairs, interrupting her father's business meeting. "You know that nice lady upstairs, Josefita? She is tired of watching cartoons. Can she please read me a story? She promised to read me a story." David Scoville ran upstairs with his daughter, but the room was empty. The little girl started to cry, asking her Dad if he knew where the nice lady had gone.

David has had other experiences with the former owner. Years earlier, he noticed some fringe at the bottom of a lampshade

Luna Mansion Restaurant

start to move although there wasn't even the slightest breeze in the air to cause the movement. When he backed up, the image of a woman, running her fingers at the bottom of the fringe, suddenly appeared before his eyes. He knew at once that it was Josefita from the photographs of her that he had seen. She was wearing a white peasant blouse, a long skirt and her hair was pulled back in a bun.

Late one evening, Mr. Scoville was walking on the lawn when he felt someone was staring at him. Glancing up toward a second floor window, he saw Josefita peering down at him. Soon after, a customer who claimed to be very sensitive to ghosts, explained to David that she felt the presence of a ghost on the second floor. She added that the female spirit liked to sit at the window so she could look out onto the lawn.

Cocktail waitresses have also seen her in the upstairs lounge. Josefita looks so human that they've mistaken her for a customer and have asked her if she'd care to order a drink.

There are two other ghosts on the premises, both looking like servants, according to one witness who has seen them.

Several have also heard them having a conversation together, although it was so muffled they couldn't make out any of the words.

Other unexplained happenings occur quite frequently at the Luna Mansion. Large swinging doors leading into the kitchen open on their own, glassware sometimes shatters when placed on a certain antique table, and doors open and shut when no one is around.

When you visit this "real" haunted mansion, and start a conversation with a lady wearing a white peasant blouse in the lounge, don't be surprised if she introduces herself as Josefita!

Address:	**Luna Mansion Restaurant**
	Main Street
	P.O. Box 789
	Los Lunas, NM 87031-0789
Phone:	(505) 865-7333
Hours:	Monday-Tuesday: Closed
	Thursday-Saturday: 5:00 pm - 9:30 pm
	Sunday: 5:00 pm - 9:00 pm

Directions: From I-40, go 23 miles south on I-25 to the Los Lunas exit. Travel east one mile to Los Lunas.

MARIA TERESA RESTAURANT

The Salvador Armijo House, now the Maria Teresa Restaurant, has been on the National Register of Historic Places since 1977. One of the finer restaurants of Albuquerque, the Maria Teresa's colorful history has been kept vividly alive throughout the years.

It is not known for certain just when the Salvador Armijo House was built. One version is that when Salvador married his cousin Paula Montoya in 1847, he built the house. The other account is that the building was built in the 1830s and Armijo purchased it from his older brother, Jose. The twelve-room hacienda was a flat-roofed, one-story dwelling with dirt floors.

Although the founders of the Maria Teresa restaurant have been deceased for years, the employees feel they are still very much alive in spirit form. Almost all of them admit to having had some type of supernatural encounter. Some restaurant patrons, as well, have had experiences with the various ghosts that linger about.

Once, when a server was approaching a seated couple, he noticed that their faces were ashen and that they were visibly shaken. They explained to him that they had just watched a woman, dressed in red, walk by them and exit through the very door the employee had entered–going right through him! The waiter merely smiled. This female spirit has been around for years. The bartenders also feel her watching over them and for some reason, the ladies' restroom is one of her favorite places.

The Armijo Room of the Maria Teresa Restaurant

Maria, another ghost, is tall, elegant and always wears a white dress with her hair pulled back with a Mexican comb. Guests, especially children, sometimes see this female specter in mirrors. When they describe her, employees know instantly that Maria has made another appearance.

A waiter working in the Armijo dining room, one of Maria's favorite places, was serving a large party. He made an unflattering statement about her and the wine glass that he was holding flew out of his hand, wine going everywhere.

A couple finishing their dinner was asked by their waiter if they cared to order dessert. They replied that they had already given their dessert order to the waitress dressed in white who had been pushing a dessert cart. The restaurant doesn't use dessert carts and female employees are always dressed in maroon.

Other paranormal activities that continue on a regular basis are sounds of laughter heard after business hours, and music playing from the old grand piano that is in the Armijo Room. Of course, when the employee goes to the room to check on the eerie sounds, he finds it dark and empty. One spirit enjoys playing tricks with the flatware in the Chacon Room and the Armijo Dining Room. More than one server, after having the table all set up for his next customer, left for only a few minutes and upon returning, finds the silverware to be in a jumble in the middle of the table.

There are also male ghosts that have been seen roaming about, both inside and on the grounds. One apparition is that of a man wearing a dark suit who appears in the Chacon Room. The image of this elderly gentleman has been seen very clearly in one of the many mirrors scattered throughout the dining area. The spirit of a dark man had been seen near an outside fountain close to a peach tree, but after the tree was cut down, he ceased coming around.

The employees are very comfortable sharing their experiences with their customers. The staff doesn't mind working alongside these ghostly inhabitants. As for the customers, well, they keep coming back hoping to step into the world of the supernatural.

Address: **Maria Teresa Restaurant**
618 Rio Grande NW
Albuquerque, NM 87104

Phone: (505) 242-3900

Hours: Monday-Sunday 11:00 am - 2:30 pm, 5:00 pm - 9:00 - pm
Lounge is open 11:00 to 9:00 daily.

Directions: From I-40, exit south on Rio Grande and travel a quarter of a mile to the restaurant.

KiMo THEATER

Oreste Bachechi used an architectural style focusing on the American Indian culture of the Southwest when he built the KiMo Theater in 1927. The plaster ceiling beams were textured to look like logs, air vents were disguised as Navajo rugs, chandeliers were shaped like war drums and panoramic murals of the Seven Cities of Cibola were painted on the walls by Carl von Hassler.

Colors were chosen carefully to represent the American Indian culture. Red representing the sun, white the approaching morning, yellow the setting sun in the west and black the darkening clouds from the north. Von Hassler mixed his own pigments for the intense colors he used, often using bichloride, a poison, in his paint.

The KiMo, which took less than a year to build, hosted such stars as Sally Rand, Gloria Swanson, Tom Mix and Ginger Rogers. Vivian Vance was an employee at the theater before becoming the zany Ethel Mertz on the "I Love Lucy Show."

Like so many other places listed on the National Directory of Historic Places, restoration is an ongoing process. To determine the original colors, several coats of paint were removed from a steer skull, door handles modeled after kachinas were duplicated from the only remaining knob and light fixtures were replicated from photographs. Now in its final stage of restoration, the balcony, the stage house and the third floor are areas of concentration.

In the mid-fifties the theater was showing an Abbot &

KiMo Theater

Costello movie when, at a particularly scary part, a six-year-old named Bobby was so frightened that he ran downstairs at the exact moment a furnace exploded. He was the only one killed.

The KiMo, also a performing arts center, has had presentations put on by a little boy poltergeist believed to be Bobby, who has a reputation for mischief, just like any mortal six-year-old. After his death, unexplainable things started happening on stage. Lights would fall, props would disappear, and some actors claim they were pushed by some invisible force.

Someone came up with the idea of erecting a shrine that would keep a 6-year-old happy and away from the stage. Cars, little trinkets, mementos from the shows, photos of children and penny candy were put at the shrine. Because they were aware of how much little boys enjoy sweets, a string was tied between water pipes in the basement on which donuts could be hung. Whether it was the toys, the sweets or the donuts, the plan worked. No more shenanigans happened on stage.

Linda Kleinfeld, an employee, admits she's never seen Bobby, "but he makes his presence known by causing a draft where there is no window or door. This sometimes causes papers to fall off a table. When these things occur I talk to him and ask him to stop and he has always obliged me."

The shrine is constantly fed, especially on opening night of each performance. Petrified donuts and little candies dangle from the string for the spirit of a little boy who was tragically killed.

Note: KiMo is a Tewa Indian word meaning mountain lion.

Address: **KiMo Theater**
423 Central NW
Albuquerque, NM 87102

Phone: (505) 764-1700

Hours: Call for hours of performances.

Directions: From I-40, exit at Sixth Street and go south to downtown Albuquerque. Turn left on Central (Route 66) and continue on to the theater. From I-25, exit on Central Avenue and travel west to the theater.

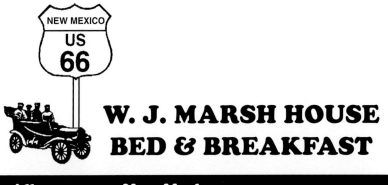

W. J. MARSH HOUSE
BED & BREAKFAST

Albuquerque, New Mexico — — — — — — — —

The W.J. Marsh House sits on a quiet street of Albuquerque's Railroad Town historic district. The calm exterior gives no hint to the activity inside, but Janice Sperling, owner of this Victorian bed and breakfast, and many of her former guests will tell you the spirits of W.J. Marsh House are very active.

Janice has owned the bed and breakfast since 1992 and has had reports of ghostly activity right from the beginning. During renovation an unsuspecting plasterer was working on the Rose Room upstairs. Imagine his amazement when two women appeared from nowhere, wearing turn-of-the-century clothing, complete with bustles and oversized hats. That was the first sighting Janice is aware of, but the ladies have returned many times and only to this room. No one knows who the women are, and it would be difficult to ever identify them, since the house has such a diverse history.

Built in 1892, it became the home of the Reverend W.J. Marsh in 1895. He lived there until 1910. Since that time, it has also been a boarding house and even rumored to have been a bordello. Based on the way the women are dressed, however, they are more likely to have been members of the Reverend's congregation than members of the bordello.

A second ghost lingers in the upstairs hallway, walking back and forth with a cane. Even though this hall is carpeted, you can hear the sound of the cane tapping on a wooden floor.

W. J. Marsh House Bed & Breakfast

The most surprising ghost here is a little boy who plays in the backyard. While Janice has not seen the spirit herself, guests at Marsh House have. They describe the boy as wearing a sailor suit with a Dutch-boy haircut. Even those who have not seen him have heard him call their names. When they turn to answer, of course, no one is there.

Address: **W. J. Marsh House Bed & Breakfast**
301 Edith SE
Albuquerque, NM

Phone: (505) 247-1001 for reservations or tours.

Directions: From I-25 North: Exit at Lead/Coal. Left on Lead (a one-way street). Travel three blocks. Turn right to Edith, travel one block. From I-25 South: Exit at Dr. Martin Luther King, Jr. Ave/ Central. Turn right on MLK. Travel four blocks to Edith. Turn left and travel four blocks. From I-40, follow the signs to I-25 South and then follow directions above to the Marsh House.

CHURCH
STREET CAFE

Nestled in the heart of Old Town Albuquerque's historic, pueblo-style buildings, in the shadow of San Felipe de Neri Catholic Church, lies the Church Street Cafe. Built in 1709, it was the home of the Ruiz family for generations. Although it is now owned by Marie Coleman, who transformed the broken building into the Cafe, it is still home to the late Sara Ruiz, a long-ago doña of the 18-room hacienda.

Sara was an unconventional woman for her time. She was known as a *curandera,* a type of healer who dabbled in herbs. While she never married, she did have children, one of whom, Rafinia, was the last resident of the Ruiz family home. After her death, the family sold the house to Marie.

Marie's first experience with Sara was during construction. The house required a great deal of work so Marie interviewed contractors. While she was taking one through the house, she could hear a woman's voice shouting at her. The voice was insistent and urgent, "Get him out of here, now!" Marie could feel the anger all around her as they moved from room to room and she rushed the contractor through with barely a chance to look around. Once outside, everything became calm. Marie had no idea who had been shouting at her, but she knew this man could not work on the house. She later learned that he was the grandson of a man Sara had been involved with long ago.

Marie finally convinced a friend, Charlie, to handle the

Church Street Cafe

work for her. She never mentioned the woman's voice she'd heard until the new contractor finally told her she'd have to do something about "that woman." "Tell her to stop kicking the buckets around," he told her. "Make her stop." Marie couldn't believe it, but Charlie was well aware of Sara. She asked just how she was supposed to stop her. He replied, "Talk to her." Marie did, and the spirit stopped kicking the buckets.

That was the beginning of their relationship. Marie believes the spirit is Sara Ruiz and Marie gives her the room and respect the doña deserves. She greets her every morning and bids her goodbye every night. Now and then, when Sara wants her attention, she tosses small pebbles at Marie. A waiter told Marie he saw the spirit of Sara in a long black dress, and customers have said they've felt a presence. When Marie's brother Jim came in to help her, he would have none of this ghost nonsense. On the first night he locked up alone, he couldn't find his keys. The door was already locked, but he needed the keys to get out. He knew where he'd put them, but they weren't there. As he began an all-out search, he heard a voice laughing. "All right, Sara," he said. "Leave me alone." He found the keys in his pocket. When he got to the door, it was unlocked. He quickly became a believer.

Address: **Church Street Cafe**
2111 Church St. NW
Albuquerque, NM 87104

Phone: (505) 247-8522

Hours: 8:00 am - 4:00 pm daily

Directions: From I-40, exit Rio Grande and go west. At the second light (Mountain St.), there is a fifth street (Romero) joining the intersection. Turn onto Romero and park along the street. Church Street is perpendicular to Romero.

Interior of the Church Street Cafe

Arizona

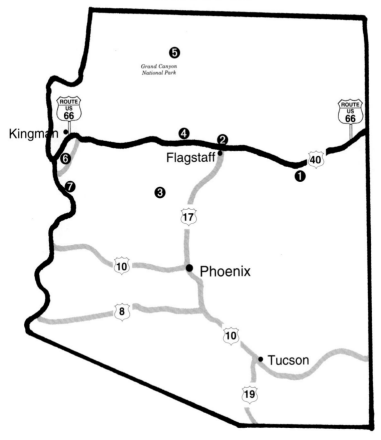

❶ **Holbrook:** *Navajo County Historic Courthouse*
❷ **Flagstaff:**
        The Museum Club
        Hotel Monte Vista
        Riordan Mansion
        Birch Tree Inn
        Comfi Cottages
❸ **Jerome:**
        The Inn at Jerome
        Jerome Grand Hotel
❹ **Williams:** *Red Garter Bed & Bakery*
❺ **Grand Canyon:** *North Rim*
❻ **Oatman:** *Oatman Hotel*
❼ **Lake Havasu:** *London Bridge*

NAVAJO COUNTY HISTORIC COURTHOUSE

The first legal hanging in Navajo County created quite a commotion. Sheriff Frank Wattron sent out 50 invitations to the execution. They were designed to resemble wedding invitations! The flowing white script with the lighthearted wording was considered "grim humor" in the November 11, 1899, edition of *The Argus,* Holbrook's local newspaper.

The invitation was quickly picked up by the Associated Press and flashed over the wire. President William McKinley sent a letter of condemnation to Governor Nathan Oakes Murphy, severely rebuking Sheriff Wattron. When Frank Wattron had the second invitations printed, they were on white paper with a black border. The envelope was also edged in black.

Both the sheriff's office and jail were located in the Navajo County Courthouse that was built in 1898. Prisoners were still being locked up in the original jail as recently as 1976. On the National Register of Historical Places, the courthouse now houses the Holbrook Chamber of Commerce Visitor's Center and Historical Museum.

George Smiley, the prisoner sentenced to be hung by Sheriff Wattron, still inhabits the old building where he spent his final days, according to Chamber and Historical Society staff. For a ghost with such a violent past, it's surprising that

Navajo County Historic Courthouse

he's so passive. Walking up and down the staircase, making noises, opening and shutting the front door and moving objects are just a few of his favorite pastimes.

The Chamber and Historical Society director, as well as the museum director, brought a Ouija board into the courthouse one Halloween and asked if there was a ghost in the building. The palette spelled out the name George. Shortly after, a horrible commotion started up; they both left immediately.

Even ghosts may like a touch of greenery now and then. One Christmas season a plant in the reception area disappeared, never to be found again. Employees were quick to put the blame on George.

Mr. Smiley may not be the only spirit that refuses to leave the old building. Driving past the Navajo County Historic Courthouse one evening, a former tourism director, his wife and son, noticed some lights on. After parking in the back of the building, the director ran inside to turn them off. As soon as he entered the building, his wife saw a female looking out of one of the windows. She rushed in to tell her husband and they searched the courthouse but could find no one. Could it have been Mary, a former prisoner who had died inside one of the holding cells, peering out?

Tourists aren't the only ones attracted to the bright postcards that are found at the information desk. Marita, the receptionist, was sitting at her desk, when she noticed the postcard rack whirling around. No one else was in the room and there was no breeze that could cause the stand to move. Could it have been George up to one of his pranks?

When you stop by to visit the Navajo County Historic Courthouse, take time to tour the former jail where both George and Mary were imprisoned. If you decide to thumb through the postcards, be on the alert. The racks may start to spin if George is in one of his feisty moods.

Address:	Navajo County Historic Courthouse 100 East Arizona Holbrook, AZ 86025
Phone:	(520) 524-6558 (800) 524-2459
Hours:	Monday - Friday 8:00 am - 5:00 pm Extended hours during the summer months

Directions: Holbrook is near the junction of I-40 and Route 77. The Navajo County Courthouse is located on old U.S. Route 66 in downtown Holbrook.

THE MUSEUM CLUB

The Museum Club was built in 1931 by Dean Eldredge to house all of his hunting trophies and large collection of rifles and Indian artifacts. The building was also used as his taxidermist shop, as well as a trading post.

In 1936, after Prohibition, a Flagstaff saddle maker named Doc Williams turned the Museum Club into a popular night club. The building was promoted as the largest log cabin in Arizona. It was built around five live ponderosa pine trees that appear to grow right out of the huge dance floor.

A mahogany bar, dating back to the 1890s, sits in the northwest corner of the Museum Club, embellishing the Old West atmosphere. More than 85 mounts are on display, so it's no wonder the locals in Flagstaff fondly call the roadhouse "The Zoo."

Enter the roadhouse through an inverted forked trunk of a native ponderosa pine tree. When the country music starts to play, swing your partner around the tree-studded dance floor. Perched above in the tree branches you'll find a bobcat, a bear, owls and even peacocks.

The owners and employees are not a bit shy admitting that ghosts are lingering around "The Zoo." In fact, they're proud that the Museum Club has a reputation of being haunted!

Don and Thelma Scott owned the Museum Club in the 1960s and seventies and unfortunately both suffered tragic

The locals in Flagstaff refer to The Museum Club
as "The Zoo."

deaths. Mr. and Mrs. Scott lived above the shop. One day while going down the stairs to the dry storage area, Mrs. Scott fell, breaking her neck. Becoming despondent, Don later took his own life in front of the fireplace.

Signs that Don and Thelma never left are evident to employees as well as guests. Footsteps and creaks coming from the upstairs where they once lived, lights flickering on and off, chairs that rock back and forth, and fires lit in the hearth when no one is around are just a few things that employees and customers are accustomed to.

These spirits do much more than the usual hijinks that ghosts generally do, though. Mrs. Scott doesn't seem to mind if you see her spirit. One tourist went to the back bar for a drink and got impatient when the lady bartender wouldn't wait on him. Tired of waiting, the customer went to the front bar to complain. Needless to say, he was surprised to learn that there wasn't any bartender on duty–the bar in the back wasn't even open. On another occasion, a customer ordered a drink for a lady that was sitting in the corner. Upon getting the drink he went to her table but she had vanished into thin air. The bar isn't the only place that Thelma is seen; she is sometimes spotted on the stairway during the day.

While in their upstairs apartment where the couple had lived, one man claims he was pinned to the floor by a friendly female ghost. I wonder how Mr. Scott feels about that?

A bartender, just starting her shift, was surprised to see the bar shelf disarrayed. Beer bottles were switched around, drink mixes were at the wrong end, and some liquor bottles had been knocked over. The bar area had already been straightened up the night before. She had no choice but to blame it on the Scotts.

Address: **The Museum Club**
3404 E. Route 66
Flagstaff, Arizona

Phone: (520) 526-9434

Hours: Daily - Noon to 1:00 am

Directions: Take the Flagstaff exit from I-40 and follow the signs to Route 66. The Museum Club is 2 1/2 miles east of downtown Flagstaff.

HOTEL MONTE VISTA

The Hotel Monte Vista, listed on the National Register of Historic Places, first opened its doors on New Year's Day, 1927. In the forties and fifties, when Western movies were popular, more than 100 were filmed in the area of Sedona and Oak Creek Canyon, both close to Flagstaff. Because there weren't any accommodations in that locality, the stars made the Monte Vista their home away from home. Rooms are named after some of the famous guests that have stayed there. A few celebrities that hold that honor are: Bing Crosby, Jane Russell, Gary Cooper and Spencer Tracy. If you're a fan of old romantic movies, you can request to spend the night in the room where a scene from Casablanca was filmed.

The hotel with a celebrated past not only has historical charm and character to offer, but a few ghosts as well. The "phantom bellboy" knocks at the Zane Grey Room announcing in a muffled voice, "room service." When the guests open the door, though, they find no one standing there, nor do they catch a glimpse of anyone dashing away down the long corridor.

"In 1970," Ellen Roberts, the desk clerk, explained, "three men robbed a nearby bank and to celebrate, they decided to stop by our lounge and have a drink–even though one of the men had been shot during their escape. While having his drink, the wounded man died, and some feel he's the spirit that's haunting this area of the building."

Hotel Monte Vista

Some repairs were needed after a fight had occurred in room 220. When his work was completed, a maintenance man turned off the light and locked the door. He returned in only five minutes to find the light back on, the television going full blast and the bed linens stripped. In the early 1980s, a strange, long-term boarder rented this room (he was known to hang raw meat from the chandelier) and when he passed away, his body wasn't discovered for two or three days. Was his ghost responsible for the upheaval that took place in the empty, locked room?

"When a father and son checked out of the Gary Cooper room, the father made the comment that during the night, he suddenly sat straight up in bed feeling like someone was staring at him," Ellen recalled. "His son started to kid him but his dad was very sincere and kept stressing that he knew someone had been watching him. The red-light district was south of the railroad tracks, not too far from the Hotel Monte Vista, and two prostitutes were murdered in that room. Another version of the story is that they died after they were thrown out the window." Could the "ladies of the night" still be looking for clients?

This hotel certainly has a variety of ghosts, all stubbornly refusing to check out. Other strange occurrences are the peculiar rings of the lobby telephone late at night, an image of a woman outside of the Zane Grey Room and sounds of a man coughing continuously through the night. If you're not lucky enough to be entertained by the permanent guests, you'll still have a good time listening to live music in the haunted cocktail lounge.

Address: **Hotel Monte Vista**
               100 N. San Francisco Street
               Flagstaff, AZ   86002
Phone: (520) 779-6971
               (800) 545-3068

Directions: From I-40, follow the signs for Highway 89 (Milton Road) into Flagstaff. Three blocks after the underpass, turn left on San Francisco St. The hotel is one block ahead, on the right. I-17 terminates at Flagstaff and becomes Milton Road. Continue as per above.

RIORDAN MANSION

Riordan Mansion is an Arizona State Historic Park. One of Arizona's most historic and elegant frontier homes, the mansion was built in 1904 by brothers Timothy & Michael Riordan. Tucked away among the Ponderosa Pines, the Riordan Mansion is located near downtown Flagstaff.

The brothers married sisters, Caroline and Elizabeth Metz, and built the 13,000 square foot home. The mansion, with two similar 5,000 square-feet of living quarters for each family, was joined together by a massive billiard room.

Even ghosts must like to have fun, especially when there is a top-of-the-line billiard table available. Arthur Riordan, son of Michael and Elizabeth, had a taste of the supernatural in that long ago era. He had declined an invitation to join his family on an outing and opted to spend the day alone. While Arthur was upstairs, he could hear billiard balls clacking together. When he went to check in the billiard room, he saw nothing and returned upstairs. Once again he heard them, but this time he returned to see the balls in motion, although no one was there. Thinking one of his relatives was somehow playing a trick on him, he put the matter out of his mind until he discovered that every member of his family was accounted for at the picnic.

The Riordans, deeply religious, had a small chapel built in the stair landing where visiting priests said mass. Caroline insisted that the light in front of a statue of Christ be lit at all

Riordan Mansion

times. One day when Caroline was away from home, a housekeeper noticed that the light was out. She tightened the light bulb and the plug. Nothing happened. Just as she was about to give up, the light started flickering on and off. Later that day the household received word that Caroline had died. Her time of death was exactly the time the chapel light flickered. Visitors and employees have claimed to have seen the ghost of Caroline looking for her daughter, Anna. A few think they have also seen apparitions of Anna, who died of polio just before she was to be married.

Sign up at the visitor's center to go on a guided tour (reservations recommended, tours on the hour). Maybe you'll be lucky enough to see billiard balls rolling around by themselves on the massive billiard table.

Address:	**Riordan Manson State Historic Park** 1300 Riordan Ranch Street Flagstaff, AZ 86001
Phone:	(520) 779-4395
Hours:	(May-Sept.) 8:00-5:00, (Oct.-Apr.) 12:30- 5:00. Open daily. $4.00 adults, $2.50 children

Directions: Exit I-40 onto Milton Road. Turn right (north) on Chambers Drive and proceed to Riordan Ranch St.

BIRCH TREE INN

Two couples, Sandy and Ed Znetko and Rodger and Donna Pettinger, are the owners of the Birch Tree Inn, having purchased it in 1988. The two-story bungalow was built in 1917 by a Chicago contractor, Joseph Waldhuas, for his large family and remained their home for 40 years.

It became a fraternity house for Sigma Tau Gamma in 1969. Sigma Chi fraternity took over just three years later. From there the house fell into disrepair as it went through a series of owners.

When Sandy, Ed, Rodger and Donna turned the house into a warm and cozy bed and breakfast, they soon discovered that their guests weren't the only ones enjoying the newly refurbished Country-Victorian house. The ghosts (Sandy's daughter-in-law, who has psychic abilities, feels there are three of them) do not favor one specific room; they've taken over the entire house.

One evening while lying in bed, Sandy realized she hadn't locked up for the night. Just before getting out of bed, she heard footsteps going up and down the stairway and assumed someone else was locking up. The next morning she found the doors securely locked. She also discovered that no one else in the household had locked the doors, each thinking that another had done so.

The ghosts, not wanting anyone to forget their presence, drop subtle hints from time to time. A lampshade fell to the floor, although there were several brackets holding it in place.

Birch Tree Inn

On another occasion, Sandy heard a crash and couldn't find the source of the noise. The next morning she discovered a cup from a closed china cabinet lying on the floor.

Sometimes friends and guests witness the ghosts' playfulness. "Folks were gathered around the kitchen table when a fork on the countertop suddenly just flew into the air," Sandy recalled, "and the lights in the kitchen sometimes flicker on and off."

The wraparound veranda is another place guests have seen firsthand why the owners hope the ghosts are there to stay. Among the wicker on the front porch is a swing. To get it in motion, just sit down and relax; the spirits do the work. Within seconds you'll be gently swinging back and forth.

Address:	**Birch Tree Inn** 824 W. Birch Avenue Flagstaff, AZ 86001-4420
Phone:	(520) 645-6805

Directions: At the intersection of I-17 and I-40, take Exit 195B (which becomes Milton Road). Follow it around to highway 180 (which becomes Humphry Street) and go left two blocks to Birch Avenue. Birch Tree Inn is on the left side of the road.

COMFI COTTAGES

In a residential area, just nine blocks from the historic district of Flagstaff, sits a cluster of six bungalows all within a few blocks of each other. The Comfi Cottages of Flagstaff were built in the 1920s and early 1930s.

For those that are seeking more than a "home away from home" getaway, always hoping for the unexpected, be sure to request the cottage at 919 N. Beaver Street.

This three-bedroom dwelling, one of the larger of the homes, was built in the 1930s. The first occupant of this cottage was the postmaster of Flagstaff. Tragically, his 18-year old daughter died of whooping cough in the 1950s.

The cottage at 919 N. Beaver Street

When Innkeepers Pat and Ed Wiebe bought the house, the girl's brother came over to pick up some of his family's belongings and related the circumstances surrounding his sister's untimely death. He mentioned that she had died in her bedroom on the second floor.

Does the dead girl's spirit still linger in this room?

Sometime later a guest staying at the home on Beaver Street mentioned that he had encountered a female ghost in the upstairs bedroom. When he said that she appeared to be in her late teens, the Wiebes couldn't help but wonder if the spirit might be that of the postmaster's daughter.

If the silent, very mellow ghosts appeal to you, here's your chance. No unexplained noises, playful antics, or cold spots in the bedroom. Just a quiet spirit who likes to return to her former home for short visits. Maybe you'll be lucky enough to catch a glimpse of her if you choose to sleep in her old bedroom.

Address: **Comfi Cottages**
1612 N. Aztec
Flagstaff, AZ 86001

Phone: (520) 774-0731 or (888) 774-0731

Directions: To get to 919 N. Beaver, exit I-40 onto Milton heading north. After crossing the railroad tracks, Milton curves east and turns into Route 66. Go past Beaver, turn left onto Leroux. Go nine blocks to Columbus and turn left. Go one block, turn right on Beaver and the haunted cottage is on your left.

THE INN
AT JEROME

In Jerome's heyday, an old-timer once boasted that there were 120 "women of the night" enjoying their profession to the fullest. Some claim that Jennie Banters, the most prominent and prosperous madam in the red-light district, was the richest woman in northern Arizona. Besides Jennie, other madams that lingered in the memories of many were Rose, Lily, Cuban Mary and Madame Pearl, who was never seen without a cigarette dangling from her lips.

Jennie Banters was also very ingenious. When a fire erupted at her home, she solicited the volunteer fire department with an unusual offer: if they would put out the fire, she would give them free lifetime passes to her establishment. It was said that the volunteers responded with superhuman energy and charged up the hill to extinguish the flames.

The Inn at Jerome has turned Madam Jennie's bordello into a turn-of-the-century Victorian inn. There are eight rooms, including one that is called "Spooks, Ghosts and Goblins."

Even though Jennie's former home is no longer a brothel, she must be happy at The Inn at Jerome, as she's never left. Her devoted pet remains behind as well.

The phantom cat appears to enjoy having the run of the house. One day while in the kitchen, the cook saw a cat dart out from beneath the grill and scamper around her feet. He vanished as fast as he had appeared. The employee searched

the area before coming to the conclusion that once again, Jennie's pet was on the prowl. When the cat curls up in a tight ball to take a nap, he leaves indentations on the beds. He is also known to brush against the legs of unsuspecting guests. If he's not in the kitchen spooking the cooks or enjoying a nice soft bed, the cat is usually roaming the hallway.

Jennie seems to enjoy being in the kitchen as well. Willow, an employee, was sitting at a table, when all of a sudden, a stack of books sitting on top of a microwave started moving by themselves before tumbling to the floor. Willow also saw an ice scoop fly off the top of the ice machine.

With eight rooms to pick from, the former madam seems to prefer the Lariat and Lace Room. She certainly keeps the maids busy when she insists on rearranging the furniture, moving objects, and rotating the ceiling fan. She is at least considerate enough to turn on the bedside radio to provide music while they're working.

There have been reports that the ghosts of prostitutes have been seen walking the streets of Jerome. Like all good madams I'm sure Jennie is still keeping a close eye on her "girls."

Address:	**The Inn at Jerome** 309 Main Street Jerome, AZ 86331
Phone:	(800) 634-5094

Directions: Jerome is between Flagstaff and Prescott, just off U.S. 89A. Turn on Hull Street and continue on Hull until you reach Main Street.

JEROME GRAND HOTEL

— — — — — — — — — — — —

The United Verde Hospital was constructed and opened by the United Verde Copper Company in 1927. The population of Jerome peaked at 15,000 during the roaring twenties, but when the mines closed, the population dwindled down to just a few hundred. The once-bustling hospital closed in 1950.

The building had a reputation of being haunted while it was still operating as a hospital. Ghostly sounds of coughing, labored breathing, moaning and cries of pain could be heard throughout the wards.

One evening a nurse on duty wasn't too happy with a gentleman she thought was bedridden. As soon as the nurse returned to the main floor after turning off all call lights, they would go on again. The patient was the only one in the ward, so upon returning upstairs, she accused him of the deed. The invalid told her he had seen a bearded man walk through the corridor and that he was the one responsible for turning the call lights back on. The nurse knew the bearded man was the ghost that had been around for quite some time.

The bizarre death of Claude Harvey remains a mystery. Was it an accident or murder? Mr. Harvey was killed when he was caught underneath the hotel elevator in 1935. Since then, lights in the elevator shaft have been seen repeatedly throughout the years. And it was not unusual to hear the creaking of the iron elevator echoing throughout the old building even though the elevator was parked at the top floor when the building was closed. The building stood vacant for forty-six years–until

Jerome Grand Hotel

1996–when it was reopened as the Jerome Grand Hotel. Not surprisingly, the hauntings have continued, some during the renovations.

In July of 1997, a guest in room thirty-two had heard talk of the room being haunted and was so afraid that he couldn't sleep. While he was just sitting there, he watched in horror as his bathroom door slowly opened all the way. He immediately retreated downstairs and remained there until daybreak.

Ghosts at the Jerome Grand Hotel can be found throughout the building. A teenager leaving the lobby pushed the double doors open, shutting them behind him. After he was out of sight, both doors reopened all the way and closed just as if the Invisible Man had been exiting the building.

Daily happenings include footsteps up and down the halls, fans starting up on their own, lights going on and off, and doors–previously locked–mysteriously unlocking themselves during the night.

Is Claude Harvey causing some of the ghostly disturbances because he can't rest in peace until the real cause of his death is known to others?

Address: **Jerome Grand Hotel**
200 Hill Street
Jerome, AZ 86331

Phone: (520) 634-8200

Directions: Jerome is between Flagstaff and Prescott, just off U.S. 89A. After entering Jerome, take the Prescott fork in the road, then turn onto Hill Street (a cobblestone road).

RED GARTER
BED & BAKERY

Many turn-of-the-century buildings still exist, as does the spirit of old Route 66, in Williams. Founded in 1882, the city was a rowdy town attracting railroad workers, Chinese laborers, loggers and cowboys.

Located on a street commonly known as "Saloon Row" sits a beautifully restored two-story Victorian Romanesque brick building. It was originally built as a saloon and bordello in 1897 by August Tetzlaff. Both businesses flourished until around 1940. Since then, the building has housed a variety of enterprises, including a Chinese restaurant and even an opium den. The building's owners were very proud of the two-story outhouse that was located in the backyard.

John Holst purchased the old bordello in the seventies, lovingly restoring the historical building so guests can capture the atmosphere of the 1890s. Once used as "cribs" by the prostitutes, the rooms have been remodeled and each of the three rooms has its own unique history: The Parlor where anxious men paced up and down waiting their turn, Madam's Room (no explanation needed), and the Honeymoon Suite, where top-of-the-line girls would lean out the front windows to wave customers in for a good time.

Because of the Red Garter's violent background, it's not surprising that there are eerie sounds on the narrow stairway which led to the bordello. A killing took place on the stairs involving one of the prostitutes and her customer. She stabbed

Red Garter Bed & Bakery

her victim in the back, causing him to fall through the front door where he died in the street. Could it be his spirit responsible for creating the ghostly haunts?

You may be lucky enough to see a ghost on the stairway or if you listen closely as you approach the second floor you may hear mysterious noises.

Address: **Red Garter Bed & Bakery**
            137 W. Railroad Ave
            PO Box 95
            Williams, AZ 86046

Phone: (520) 635-1484
            (800) 328-1484

Directions: Williams is 32 miles west of Flagstaff off of I-40. Exit south at 163, and follow Old Route 66 (Railroad Avenue), which is one-way, to the Red Garter Bed & Bakery.

GRAND CANYON

The Grand Canyon was proclaimed a Forest Reserve in 1893, a National Monument in 1908 and finally in 1919 it became a National Park. It includes 1,892 square miles and receives more than three million visitors annually.

The last place you would expect a ghost to be roaming about would be the Grand Canyon. Ghosts are usually associated with large, old buildings or cemeteries with tombstones ready to topple over with the help of just a slight breeze, certainly not at the North Rim of the Grand Canyon surrounded by miles of lush, thick forest with the San Francisco Peaks for a backdrop. The Wandering Woman can be seen roaming this area–possibly because it is so quiet and remote, or perhaps because she is still searching for her family.

The Wandering Woman hung herself in a lodge on the North Rim after learning that her husband and son were killed in a hiking accident in the canyon. The lodge burned down in 1926 but has since been rebuilt.

She has been seen by many employees on the North Kaibab Trail wearing a white robe dotted with pink and blue flowers and always with a shawl covering her head. The Wandering Woman has also been seen standing in a doorway of the forest ranger's quarters.

It's not only an adult who lingers at the Grand Canyon, but the spirits of children as well. Workers have seen children playing on swings, and they watched as one little girl pushed a merry-go-round and then disappeared before their eyes. The playground has since been torn down but, hopefully, these spirits have found other merry-go-rounds and swings they can play on.

Other unusual happenings occurring at the Grand Canyon include noises of unknown origin and objects moving on the desks of office workers. A female employee, staying at one of the dorms, claims to have seen her pillow levitate above her bed. Late at night, balls of lights can be seen in the distance. What causes them is a mystery.

If you're ever on a trail at the North Rim, don't be surprised if you pass a woman dressed in white or see children frolicking at a distance that suddenly vanish before your eyes.

Address: **Grand Canyon National Park**
Grand Canyon, AZ 86046

Phone: (520) 638-7779 for information

Directions: From Flagstaff, take Highway 89 north and then west to Jacob Lake. Take Highway 67 south to the North Rim.

OATMAN HOTEL & RESTAURANT

The weathered old mining town of Oatman, which sits in the western foothills of the Black Mountains, is located 28 miles southwest of Kingman. The road–Route 66–leading to this historic town, twists and dips through a glorious canyon full of chollas, prickly pears, and barrel cactus. Long-deserted mine shafts can be seen scattered about.

Route 66 runs down Main Street with old buildings, restaurants, saloons and gift shops lining both sides. Oatman is famous for its friendly burros that amble down main street, nuzzling for handouts.

Another thing the town is famous for is Oatie, a mischievous ghost that resides at the Oatman Hotel. The two-story adobe building, listed on the National Register of Historic Buildings, was constructed in 1921.

Locals believe that Oatie is the bewildered spirit of a cowboy who became a drunk because he missed his family back in Ireland. He died in 1930 in a trash heap behind the hotel, where he lay for two days before his body was kicked into a shallow grave.

Missy, a former employee, thought Oatie was actually a miner. She said his spirit communicated with her and said that his name was Charlie. Regardless of his name and if he was a cowboy or a miner (or both), the fact remains that he is a friendly spirit that everyone enjoys having around.

Oatman Hotel & Restaurant

Oatie definitely doesn't like the window in his old room closed. The window remains opened, no matter how many times it's shut. Oatie's old pink chenille bedspread has to be neat and tidy. If he isn't pleased with the way the bed is made up, he changes it to suit himself.

In July of 1996, a guest staying in Oatie's room asked to be moved elsewhere. He complained that his room was icy cold even though the temperature that day reached 105! Another guest reported that he had seen the doorknob turn several times on its own.

A journalist requested this specific room because it was haunted. Oatie came through for him. Footsteps were heard and the room suddenly turned icy cold. Sounds of coins clinking and a deck of cards being shuffled made the reporter think that he was hearing a poker game. The noises were coming from only inches above his head; so close he knew the other guests on the floor above him weren't responsible for the late night activity.

According to Missy, Oatie also makes sure that a certain page of the guest book, located on an antique table, is opened at all times. The pages flip by themselves until his favorite page is on top.

Oatie isn't the only ghost that lingers about. Clark Gable and Carol Lombard spent their wedding night here. Guests and employees claim to hear laughter and whispers coming from the honeymoon suite. A professional photographer recently took a photo of the supposedly empty room and when the film was developed, found the ghostly image of a man.

The downstairs area is also populated by playful spirits, especially in the bar area. A bartender had five or six pennies at the end of the counter when suddenly they all flew off. Drinking glasses have also been seen flying through the air.

Other unexplainable things that have happened are toilets flushing in empty bathrooms and lights on in rooms where there aren't any switches. Also, footprints appear from nowhere on freshly scrubbed floors.

If you're ever in the mood to play a hand of cards, spend the night in Oatie's old room. Who knows, maybe he'll even let you shuffle the cards!

Address: **Oatman Hotel & Restaurant**
181 Main, Route 66
Oatman, AZ 86433

Phone: (520) 768-4408

Directions: From Kingman, take Route 66 southwest for 26 miles to Oatman.

LONDON BRIDGE

The verse "London Bridge is falling down," literally came about when the famous bridge started sinking into the River Thames due to the steady increase of city traffic. When the well-known landmark was put up for sale in 1962, the late Robert McCulloch, an Arizona developer, snapped it up.

The bridge was dismantled and the stones were coded with four numbers. The first number indicated the span, the second marked the row of stones and the next two numbers showed its position in the row. Boats carrying the bits and pieces of the bridge docked at Long Beach, California, and the bricks were then trucked to Lake Havasu.

Reassembled like a giant jigsaw puzzle, forty craftsmen worked from a copy of the original plans drawn by John Rennie in 1824. It took four years to re-create the 130,000 tons of granite. A mile-long channel separating the airport island from the shore was excavated beneath it. Dedication by the Lord Mayor of London took place October 10, 1971.

Under and around its five arches is an authentic English village with Tudor-style shops and eateries. The charming tourist attraction is complete with an English double-decker bus, a red telephone call box and pub.

During the opening ceremony, one woman noticed four figures that were strolling across the bridge. As they were dressed in Victorian attire she thought it was a part of the dedication ceremony to have townsfolk dressed in costumes from that era. She and other onlookers soon realized that what

London Bridge
Photo courtesy Curtis A. Westermeyer

they were looking at was unreal! These were specters re-creating their walks of yesterday. The packing crates that came across the Atlantic apparently carried more than the stones for the London Bridge, they contained some British ghosts as well!

The ghosts, a long way from home, still surface from time to time. The most frequent reports are of a man and a woman ambling across the bridge seemingly unaware of their sur-roundings. Those that have been lucky enough to spot these spirits are usually disappointed if they try to approach them. By the time they reach them, the ghosts vanish into thin air. However, a few of the viewers have actually been bumped by an invisible entity. Some have even seen the ghosts immediately after this contact but only for a fraction of a second.

So when you go, be careful not to get pushed off London Bridge by an unseen spirit!

Information: **Lake Havasu Tourism Bureau**

Phone: (800) 2-HAVASU

Directions: From I-40, take exit 9 (Highway 95) south to Lake Havasu City.

Southern California

❶ **Calico:** *Calico Ghost Town*
❷ **Monrovia:** *Aztec Hotel*
❸ **Pasadena:**
     Pasadena Playhouse
     Colorado Street Bridge
❹ **San Gabriel:** *San Gabriel Civic Auditorium*
❺ **Newbury Park:** *Stagecoach Inn Museum*
❻ **Los Angeles:** *Oban Hotel*
❼ **Hollywood:** *Roosevelt Hotel*
❽ **Wilmington:** *Drum Barracks*
❾ **Rancho Palos Verde:** *Point Vincente Lighthouse*
❿ **Santa Monica:** *Georgian Hotel*

CALICO
GHOST TOWN

– – – – – – – – – – – – – –

The mining camp of Calico, located ten miles east of Barstow, was founded in March of 1881 when silver was discovered there. The multicolored mountains behind the town, sporting reds, whites, purples and greens of the various minerals, prompted the miners to name the town Calico because these colors were found in calico skirts of the period.

In its heyday, the town had 1200 residents and boasted 22 saloons, many of which remained opened 24 hours a day. Like other mining towns of this period, Calico had its red-light district. The houses with their "fallen angels" were found toward the south end of the mining camp, but within its main business district.

Calico has come alive once again as a commercialized county park where visitors can relive old west history for themselves. Five of the many buildings scattered throughout the ghost town are original. The Park Office once housed a bordello.

A few ghosts chose to linger behind in this old boom town. Lucy B. Lane still inhabits her old house, now the Lane Home Needlepoint Store. Lucy's favorite wicker chair in her bedroom rocks back and forth on its own. If her chair is moved to a different location, it is always found where Lucy had kept it; facing the front window. Does she still pass the time by watching people stroll past her home?

Calico Ghost Town

On more than one occasion, a clerk has opened the store in the morning to find pictures, normally hanging on the wall, piled in the middle of the floor. Had they dropped on their own, they would have fallen straight down, not to the middle of the room. Surprisingly, the frames and glass have always been intact.

Clerks working in the store after business hours sometimes hear noises and movement, but they can never find the source of the sounds. One employee appreciates the fact that this was, after all, Lucy's house, and greets her each morning and tells her goodnight as she closes up the business.

Lil's Saloon, an original building, has a variety of ghosts that prefer to be heard, not seen. While sitting on the bench waiting for the doors to be opened, several tourists were surprised to hear the sounds of an old-style piano and a rowdy crowd coming from the inside of the building. Peering through the windows, they found the old watering hole empty.

Employees getting ready to close up Lil's sometimes hear the jingle of spurs and other unexplained sounds. They can never track down the origin of the noise.

A former historian of Calico saw the spirit of a pale lady, dressed in Spanish white lace, on the outskirts of town. While walking toward her, he watched with astonished eyes as she disappeared when he was only 100 yards away.

A couple visiting the old schoolhouse in 1990 spoke to a tall woman dressed in 1890s garb. She explained to them that she had been the last teacher at Calico. They had pictures taken with the woman, but when the film was developed only the man and woman were in the photograph. Calico's last teacher–Mrs. Margaret Olivier–passed away in 1932. She was buried at Calico at her own request. Did Margaret love teaching so much that her career carried over into her afterlife?

Address:	**Calico Ghost Town Regional Park** P.O. Box 638 Yermo, CA 92398
Phone:	(800) 862-2542
Hours:	Daily 8 am - dusk, closed Christmas Day Shops are opened from 9am - 5pm

Directions: From Barstow, travel northeast on I-15 for about 10 minutes. Exit I-15 at Ghost Town Road and follow the signs.

AZTEC HOTEL

This historical landmark, built in 1924, is an example of some of the architectural oddities used by businesses to lure people in from Route 66. The Aztec Hotel, two stories high, is probably the highlight of Robert Stacy-Judd's career. The hotel bursts with enthusiastic pre-Columbian exaggerations which Robert, a trendy architect, considered a distinguished basis for a true style of the southwest.

Not much is known about the history of the Aztec Hotel, except that it had been a hotel, a speakeasy and–for a time–a bordello. Once again, it serves as a hotel.

In the twenties or thirties a tragic accident occurred to a young couple in room 120. During their lovemaking, the wife fell off the bed and hit her head on the radiator, causing her death. Every room located west of 120, which includes rooms 118, 116, 114, etcetera, has been without heat since the misfortune. Time and time again, the heating system is checked out, but it is always found to be in working order.

Female ghosts appear to haunt the ladies room in the lobby across from the main desk. They open and shut locked doors just before an icy chill descends over the room.

In July of 1997 a baffling occurrence happened at the billiard and dart supply store located in the northeast corner of the building. At three in the morning, the sensor alarms in the store went off. The local police came to the scene as did the alarm company and the owner of the store. Upon entering the establishment, they found nothing. The store is equipped with

Aztec Hotel
Photo courtesy Kieran J. Waugh

a three-way system. One alarm is on the doors, the second on the windows, and the third, the sensors, are throughout the interior. The sensors were the only alarm to go off. There were no earthquakes of any size that morning, nor did any other sensor alarms in the area go off. The alarm company insisted that even if a cat had snuck into the store, it wouldn't have enough body mass to activate the alarm. After a thorough check by all present, they concluded there was no physical reason or mechanical malfunction for this to have happened. Could it have been a couple of guys from the days of the speakeasy having a friendly game of darts?

Even though the Aztec was closed down for a period of time, becoming sorely neglected, some spirits are determined to stay, especially since the hotel has been refurbished.

Address:	**Aztec Hotel** 311 West Foothill Boulevard Monrovia, CA 91016
Phone:	(626) 358-3231

Directions: Take I-210 Exit (Myrtle) north to Foothill Boulevard. Turn left and proceed to the Aztec.

PASADENA PLAYHOUSE

The Playhouse, built in 1925 and registered as a Historical Landmark, was designed by Elmer Grey. Although not the first theater in the state, it is considered the official State Theater of California. It is the oldest theatrical production organization in the West.

Restored in 1986, Mainstage seats 750; the old Balcony Theater is undergoing renovation; the Patio Theater has been converted into a restaurant.

Gilmor Brown, the founder, had passageways built into the Pasadena Playhouse so he could watch the rehearsals without anyone knowing of his presence. He was the driving force behind the theater before passing away in 1959. He knows the show must go on, so his spirit has stayed on to make sure it does.

Although Gilmor hasn't been physically seen, everyone associated with the Pasadena Playhouse is aware of his benign spirit. His favorite area, of course, is still the stage.

When the Pasadena Playhouse Actors Workshops, co-founded by Jill Maina Capps, arrived "back home" at the Playhouse in early 1990, strange occurrences–which began shortly after Gilmor's death–started up again. Teachers and students reported "a presence" in remote nooks and crannies as well as while they were rehearsing late. The incidents happened so often that Ms. Capps felt it prudent to explain the

Pasadena Playhouse
Photo courtesy Kieran J. Waugh

legend of Gilmor's ghost at every new student assembly.

Many years ago, while she herself was a student at the Pasadena Playhouse College of Theater Arts, Jill was feeling jumpy as she worked late one evening in the empty Patio Theater. However, she continued to paint the scenery on stage. She heard a door open and just as quickly shut. Alarmed, she checked outside and found no one; then,she remembered, Mr. Brown's spirit was there protecting her and was responsible for the door opening and shutting. She relaxed.

What could have been a tragic accident was avoided thanks to their late founder. A tech student, Kathy Herbert, was working on some scenery on Mainstage when she heard a sound. Whipping around to see what caused the noise, she glanced up just in time to see a counterweight start to fall. She had only seconds to jump to safety. The counterweight, which is used to lower and raise the scenery, had somehow gotten loose, causing it to fall. There was never a question as to whom or what made the warning sound to alert Kathy.

The Pasadena Playhouse was close to being destroyed when David Houk and several other gentlemen, along with the City of Pasadena, went into partnership and renovated it.

David's first artistic director, Jessica Meyerson, had done theatrical work in Malaysia. When she heard about the spirit of Gilmor Brown, she decided she didn't want to work alongside of a spirit. Without checking with anyone first, she brought in a group of people and performed an exorcism rite she had learned in the South Seas.

Two weeks later she attended her first meeting of the Pasadena Playhouse Alumni and Associates where she told everyone about the exorcism she had performed to get rid of their beloved spirit.

"We all nearly dropped over, very upset," Jill explained. "Two or three days later, when there was another Gilmor incident, we all breathed a sigh of relief knowing he was still with us."

Sadly, when the 1994 earthquake took its toll, it was decided that the workshops could no longer operate out of the Playhouse. Since then no one has reported a "visitation," but Jill believes that Gilmor must simply be "lying doggo" until the next batch of eager students grace his halls.

Address:	**Pasadena Playhouse**
	39 South El Molino
	Pasadena, CA 91101
Phone:	(626) 356-7529 or 1-800-233-3123
Hours:	Please call for schedules

Directions: Take Lake Avenue south from I-210 to El Molino, the Playhouse is 3 blocks west.

COLORADO STREET BRIDGE

The Colorado Street Bridge, on the original Route 66, is called the most romantic and beautiful bridge in southern California. Others, however, refer to it as "Suicide Bridge." Whatever name one chooses to call it, everyone agrees that a drive across this national treasure is a must.

The structure, finished in 1913, was the highest concrete bridge in the world, soaring to a height of 144 feet. One unusual feature is the curve of the nine arched spans across the arroyo. The engineers built it with a graceful curve, not for artistic show but for structural purposes.

Colorado Street Bridge
Photo courtesy Kieran J. Waugh

Famous and not-so-famous people have strolled along the bridge. William Holden was known to walk on his hands along the railing. Albert Einstein would walk the length of the bridge during his teaching days at Cal Tech.

The Colorado Street Bridge has even been used in movies. In the film "Roman Scandals," Eddie Cantor drove a chariot through the arches. On Flag Day in 1926, pilot Art Coebel flew a biplane under the bridge with a woman hanging from each wing in a stunt for a Paramount newsreel.

Sadly, the Colorado Street Bridge is also famous for numerous suicides that have occurred. Pasadena police estimate the number of unhappy people taking their lives from this monument to be about 100. Other sources state the number to be considerably higher–closer to 200.

The first recorded suicide happened in 1919, six years after the bridge opened. During the crash of 1929 and the depression-era of the thirties, the number of distraught people leaping to their deaths multiplied. Were these mentally disturbed residents with a self-destruct desire, or was there a force that encouraged them?

Some feel that the spirit of a departed construction worker may have lured these unhappy people to their demise. When the bridge was under construction, a worker lost his footing and fell into the wet concrete that was filling a form for one of the huge supporting pillars. No one realized what had happened until much later, and it was decided that his body could not be removed. When the spirit of this deceased laborer is lingering about though, he does warn everyone in the area by turning the street lights blue!

This account hasn't been substantiated and some feel it's just a legend. However, you can't help but wonder if those who are aware of this story would walk across the Colorado Street Bridge if they glanced up and saw the street lights turn blue. Would you?

Address: **Colorado Street Bridge**
Colorado Street
Pasadena, CA

Directions: On Colorado Boulevard, west of Orange Grove.

SAN GABRIEL CIVIC AUDITORIUM

San Gabriel, California — — — — — — — — — —

The Mission Playhouse, now the San Gabriel Civic Auditorium, was built in the 1920s specifically for the creation of the "Mission Play" written by John Steven McGroarty. The production was the dramatization of the history and development of the missions and the conversion of the Indians to Catholicism. The building was never intended to be used for any other purpose. It was closed in 1933 after 3,000 performances.

After the building was once again opened for theatrical productions, it was soon discovered that there was a guest who loved the performances so much he never left. From the start it was assumed that the spirit was that of John Steven McGroarty, or simply Uncle John.

Throughout the years, some members of the audience sitting on the right side of the house have asked to be seated elsewhere as they felt something was there, "a presence or a spirit" is how they described their uncomfortable feelings. And it's common to hear footsteps throughout the empty building while employees are locking up at night.

A big canvas drop hanging on the stage is the last remaining remnant of the "Mission Play." The drop is on a wooden batten and hangs on two hemp ropes. From time to time it swings back and forth, swaying on just one side. The manager, Bill Shaw, like many others, feels that Uncle John sits on the batten pushing the drop back and forth, especially when he is pleased with a performance.

San Gabriel Civic Auditorium

In the late sixties or early seventies, a seance was held to find out more about the ghost that was on the premises. Right away the medium felt a presence but told the group that their ghost wasn't the late John Steven McGroarty, as had been assumed. The spirit instead belonged to Marcus Aguilar.

Mr. Aguilar, the stage manager in the last days of the "Mission Play," decided to take a job in New York. After sending his family to their new home by train, he started cross-country in their truck getting as far as Las Vegas when he changed his mind. Realizing his heart was in San Gabriel, he turned around and headed back. En route to California, he had a head-on collision with a construction truck. Marcus was killed instantly when rebar went through the windshield and his face.

Years later, a touring production of "Peter Pan" put on by a youth group, was being performed at the San Gabriel Civic Auditorium. Several of the children knew if a performance was good, the drop would swing back and forth, and were disappointed when this didn't happen with their show. Thirty minutes before their last performance, the producer, director and stage manager were standing on the stage landing. Barbara, an unexpected visitor from England, walked in the back door. She explained that she was touring the United States on a grant to study youth theater programs. When she walked on the landing, the drop started to swing madly while the kids went wild. She asked what the commotion was all about and the director explained that their ghost was letting them know how happy he was with the show.

"Oh, you must mean the bloke that's sitting up there on the drop, holding onto the rope. He's wearing a tweed coat and a hat, looking all around." she said. Barbara then started talking to him as the drop continued to swing back and forth.

Before leaving, Barbara was taken to the front office to thumb through some old photos in hope of identifying the ghost. After a while she pointed Marcus out in a group shot, but explained that Mr. Aguilar had a blank spot where his face should have been. It took only a minute before the group realized that the picture reflected his face the way it was after it was destroyed in the tragic automobile accident.

If you're ever lucky enough to watch a performance in this beautiful historic building, keep a close eye on the drop. If it's swinging, you'll know that Mr. Aguilar is still overseeing productions and is giving the play a "thumbs up."

Address:	**San Gabriel Civic Auditorium**
	320 South Mission Drive
	San Gabriel, CA 91776
Phone:	(626) 308-2865
Hours:	Call ahead for production times.

Directions: Exit I-10 onto San Gabriel Boulevard and follow the signs to the auditorium.

STAGECOACH INN MUSEUM

The Grand Union Hotel, an important stop for weary travelers on the stage route between Los Angeles and Santa Barbara, first opened its doors on July 4, 1876. After it ceased being a hotel in 1906, it was used as a church, school, military academy and a tea room.

The former inn housed the Tantony Gift Shop from 1952 until 1965. This very expensive and fashionable boutique, with a reputation of carrying exotic merchandise, had clientele patronizing the store from as far away as Los Angeles.

After the gift shop closed down, the Stagecoach Inn Museum opened up in the Old Union Hotel. When a new freeway was built in the area, the original redwood frame building was forced to relocate a half mile further back from the original site. Their ghosts moved right along as well.

Ghosts generally appear to be more active after major renovations but the spirits here didn't wait until construction was finished! A workman was hit on the head by a two-by-four and on another occasion, several boards came flying out of a second-story window. In both cases, no one was around who could have been the culprit.

A night watchman also reported hearing footsteps at the top of the landing every night at the same time. His dogs refused to go up the stairs when the footsteps could be heard. Once he accepted the sounds and began talking with the ghost, they ended.

Stagecoach Inn Museum

Sybil Leek, a psychic, told staff members about Pierre Devon, their resident ghost. She had come to the Stagecoach Inn in 1966 along with a parapsychology author, the museum's director, a reporter and a photographer to investigate what was behind the strange disturbances. Pierre, she reported, was murdered in one of the bedrooms between 1882 and 1889. She described him as a traveler who was headed to Los Angeles when he was killed. She thought that Pierre was a stocky man with a beard.

Janet Main, assistant director of the Stagecoach Inn, had her first experience with Pierre that same year. While working alone on the first floor, she heard noises coming from the second floor, went upstairs, didn't find anything and returned downstairs. This happened several times until Janet finally called out, "Pierre–Shut up! I'm busy." The noises, she reported, instantly stopped.

Pierre came to Janet's rescue when she and an employee from the Recreation and Parks District couldn't get the key to open the inn's door. After several tries she finally said jokingly, "Pierre, come on now. I've had enough of this. For heaven's sakes open the door!" She then tried the key again and the door opened.

In 1970 a fire completely destroyed the Stagecoach Inn and most of it's historic collection. Several pictures taken at the scene show a man's face seen above the thick, billowing smoke. Pierre?

The Stagecoach Inn was completely rebuilt after the fire, and the ghosts still remain. Reports of children laughing when there are none around, music coming from nowhere, a little boy ghost that has been seen and auras of freezing chills are just a few signs that the spirits have no intention of leaving.

Pierre isn't the least bit shy around visitors. If you feel a draft when going upstairs, you'll know he's around. He's even been spotted (his back, that is) going into one of the rooms on the upper level. The staff would certainly be disappointed if Pierre ever decided to take up residence elsewhere—they've grown fond of this bearded gentleman.

Address:	**Stagecoach Inn Museum** 51 S. Ventu Park Road Newbury Park, CA 91320
Phone:	(805) 498-9441
Hours:	Wednesday-Sunday 1:00 pm-4:00 pm for docent-led tours. Entire complex open on Sunday 1:00 pm - 4:00 pm. Closed Easter, Thanksgiving, Christmas and New Year's Day

Directions: On U.S. Hwy. 101 (Ventura Freeway) midway between Ventura and Los Angeles, exit south on Ventu Park Road and travel 1/2 mile to the museum.

OBAN HOTEL

Built in the 1930s, the Oban Hotel did not attract the rich and famous with grand splendor. Instead, this plain hotel catered to the unknowns with little money who were flocking into the Golden State, hoping to make it into show business.

Three former guests must be happy with the Oban, as they've never checked out. The employees feel the ghosts all live in the basement, though their spirits venture up occasionally.

On February 18, 1933, the *Los Angeles Times* reported that Charles Love, a stunt man and a double for Harry Langdon, shot himself in his room at the Oban. One owner of the hotel felt that Love was murdered. Could he be one of the ghosts roaming the hotel, a restless spirit wrongly accused of suicide?

A cleaning lady refuses to step into rooms 311 and 312, claiming she feels she is never alone. In 1997, a male guest who had stayed in room 311 came to the front desk, in hysterics. Diana Rodriquez, the manager, explained. "He claimed that while he was sleeping next to his wife, he was raped during the night by an unseen presence. He kept insisting that he hadn't been hallucinating. He checked out right then. He was frantic."

Guests are always complaining that they can hear people pacing back and forth in the hallway, but when they open their doors they never see anyone. As with most haunted buildings, strange noises occur on a daily basis.

Ms. Rodriquez had an eerie experience in the basement. "It was three in the morning when I heard my son's name called out, even though I was alone. I said I would be leaving as soon

Oban Hotel
Photo courtesy Kieran J. Waugh

as I finished drying the clothes and got out of there quickly."

One manager is very familiar with the Oban, as his father was a previous owner. As a small child he was in the basement when something scared him so much he wouldn't go down there again for several months. He still refuses to discuss what it was that frightened him as a youngster.

Rarely do these ghosts make visible appearances, but Diana was lucky enough to catch a glimpse of one on two occasions. Both times an older lady dressed in white appeared before her in a large mirror located in the hallway. Although there were several others in the immediate area, she was the only one fortunate enough to have seen her.

Address: **Oban Hotel**
6364 Yucca Street
Los Angeles, Ca 90028

Phone: (323) 466-0524

Directions: Follow U.S. Highway 101 (Hollywood Freeway) east to the N. Cahuenga exit. Continue on Cahuenga to Yucca Street, turn left and continue to the Oban Hotel.

HOLLYWOOD ROOSEVELT HOTEL

Hollywood, California — — — — — — — — — —

In its heyday, the Roosevelt Hotel personified Hollywood. Opening in 1927 across the street from Mann's Chinese Theater, it quickly became a center of Hollywood society. It hosted post-screening parties, meetings of the academy and the first Academy Award presentations. It was home to such actors as Rudy Vallee and David Niven. Is it any wonder that ghosts of such a past choose to linger here and re-live those exciting days? In fact, the Hollywood Roosevelt is home to so many ghosts, management keeps a list and invites guests to add to it when they have an experience of their own. So here's a chance to see a ghost you might actually recognize.

In 1984, the hotel was restored to the tune of 1.2 million dollars, and the work must have pleased the spirits of the actors from the past because many of them are back. Some of the ghostly phenomena of the hotel include phone calls from an unfinished room that didn't have a phone yet, a ghost who pushed a maid into a supply closet, and a strange man in a white suit who walked through a door and vanished. This may have been the same man seen by a couple of guests while they were strolling along the mezzanine. They saw him standing next to a piano in the Blossom Room. After greeting him and receiving no response they walked closer only to watch him disappear.

Room 928 seems to be the most active, spiritually speaking. Operators still get calls about "noisy people" in that room. When security investigates, the room is always empty. When

The Marilyn Monroe mirror at the Hollywood Roosevelt

Montgomery Clift was making "From Here to Eternity," he stayed in room 928 for three months and spent much of his time pacing up and down the hall outside the room, rehearsing his lines. Both employees and guests have reported something brushing by their arms when they pass.

One of the most interesting hauntings is in a mirror, currently located at the lower level elevator landing. It once belonged to Marilyn Monroe and was moved from her suite to its current location. The blonde, female ghost in the mirror was first seen by a hotel employee while dusting it. Is it the ghost of Marilyn Monroe? Drop in at the Hollywood Roosevelt and take a look for yourself.

Address: **Hollywood Roosevelt Hotel**
7000 Hollywood Blvd.
Hollywood, CA 90028

Phone: (323) 466-7000

Directions: From the Hollywood Freeway, take the Sunset Boulevard Exit south to Orange. Turn right and travel 2 blocks to the hotel parking lot.

DRUM BARRACKS

The Drum Barracks Civil War Museum and Research Library was, between the years 1861 and 1871, an Army headquarters for the Southwest. The old outpost, which was also called Camp Drum, originally had 19 structures situated on the 60 acres of land belonging to the U. S. Army. The only remaining building, which now houses the museum, served as the "Unaccompanied Officers' Quarters" of the camp.

A group of community workers saved the building from being demolished in the early 1960s and in 1986 it was opened as a nationally-accredited museum. The old structure came back to life in more ways than one.

Employees, volunteers and visitors have all experienced a touch of the supernatural in what was once an important Army headquarters. The more prevalent spirits are: Col. James Curtis, his wife Maria and, Jonathon, age five or six.

Colonel Curtis certainly made one city worker a believer in ghosts. The exterminator, hunched under the sink in the kitchen, heard footsteps, but didn't pay any attention until he was asked if he had seen Maria. When he turned around to tell him he hadn't seen anyone, he was a little taken aback when he saw that the man was in full military uniform from the Civil War era. While the pest control operator finished his job, his visitor disappeared. As he was leaving, he mentioned to the caretaker the conversation with one of the workers and how he

Drum Barracks

must take his job seriously enough to dress in period clothing. The caretaker informed him he had just seen the ghost of Col. James Curtis who must have been looking for his wife.

The ghostly mistress of the Drum Barracks is the Colonel's wife, Maria. Her manifestation first appeared on the balcony in the 1920s and was seen by a neighbor living across the street. More than seventy years later, he still catches glimpses of Maria.

Vince Manchester, a caretaker and protector of the property from 1965 to 1977, was another of the lucky ones to have seen the lovely dark-haired spirit. From the darkened hallway Vince saw a dim shape move on the upper part of the stairway, six or seven steps from the top. He was able to make out the form of a young woman in a long, full dress. But, much to his disappointment, when he shined his flashlight in her direction, she disappeared.

In 1991, Barbara Connors, a well-known psychic, also caught a glimpse of Maria on the stairs. She described her as about 5' 4", long beautiful black hair, dark complexion, with a frail frame. The clothing she was wearing, a hoop skirt and apron, dated from the mid-1800s.

Not much is known about Jonathon, the energetic little boy

who loved playing with his ball. Victor, a tour guide, related that they feel Jonathon's mother was deceased and that his father brought Jonathon to the Drum Barracks as a temporary home. Unfortunately, shortly after his arrival, the little boy died of smallpox. Jonathon continues to bounce his ball against an upstairs wall. When the staff gets tired of the thumping noise, they call up to him to stop and it is soon quiet again.

Although the spirits don't appear on a daily basis, other things happen to keep everyone at the Drum Barracks on their toes. A deck of old-fashioned playing cards laid out on an 1841 oak table in the parlor room might be in a different position a few hours later. Also the window shades don't stay down very long because the permanent residents prefer that the rooms should be filled with sunlight.

When Marge O'Brien, the director, discovered artifacts that had been on an old table had been scattered on the floor one morning, she remarked out loud, "Well, that's enough of that nonsense!" The spirits must have been listening; the items have been left alone.

Distinctive odors drifting throughout the museum are a pleasant reminder for the staff that spirits are nearby. The smell of candle wax coming from the parlor, whiffs of burnt tobacco in one of the bedrooms and the odor of lilac perfume in the library occur quite often.

Is Colonel Curtis still in command of his old outpost?

Address:	**Drum Barracks**
	1052 Banning Boulevard
	Wilmington, CA 90744
Phone:	(310) 548-7509
Hours:	Daily 9 am to 3 pm. Weekends 10 am to 4 pm.

Directions: From I-110 exit right on the Pacific Coast Highway (from Highway 710 exit left). Continue to North Avalon Boulevard. Turn right on Avalon and follow it to East Denni. Turn left and continue on East Denni to the corner of East Denni and Banning Boulevard.

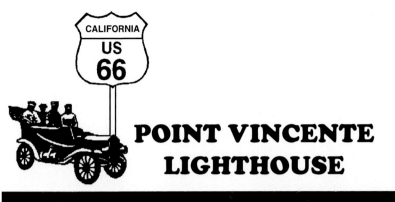

POINT VINCENTE LIGHTHOUSE

The U.S. Coast Guard's Point Vincente Lighthouse on the Palos Verdes Peninsula guided ships off the jagged coast since May 1, 1926, when it first went into service. The lighthouse was automated in 1971, ending the need for any crews or civilian keepers. This picturesque, 67-foot lighthouse can be seen from up to 20 miles at sea.

The spirit of a young woman made her first appearance when the landward side of the lens room was given a coat of white paint following World War II. No one knows for sure who she is or why she returned.

One popular version is that her lover drowned in a shipwreck off the point. When she heard the news she leaped to her death by jumping off a high cliff. Wearing a long, flowing gown, she has been seen running to the edge of the cliff or pacing the catwalk around the tower at night, maybe hoping her lover will join her.

Another account is that the female spirit is a lighthouse keeper's wife who was killed when she fell from a nearby cliff during a dense fog. The misty figure, with long, tangled hair, has been seen walking the grounds after dark.

Perhaps there are actually two apparitions wandering the area: a lovesick maiden and the deceased wife of a lighthouse keeper?

Point Vincente Lighthouse

Officially, the beautiful ghostly phantom hasn't been seen since 1955 when thicker paint was applied to the same area on the lens room. The new coat of paint may have ended her nightly prowling, but she still draws in many ghost hunters hoping to catch a glimpse of her old-fashioned gown blowing in the wind.

Dedicated as a historical site on November 17, 1979, the Point Vincente Lighthouse isn't opened without an appointment, but if you call in advance, arrangements can be made for a tour. The Point Vincente Interpretive Center, a museum and whale-watching site, sits next to the lighthouse.

Don't be surprised to find yourself in the company of a young woman with long tangled hair while you're enjoying the view at the edge of the cliff!

Address: **Point Vincente Lighthouse**
31501 Palos Verdes Drive West
Rancho Palos Verdes, CA 90274

Phone: (310) 541-0334 Call for appointments.

Directions: From the Pacific Coast Highway, take Hawthorne Boulevard south. Follow Hawthorne Boulevard until it ends at Palos Verdes Drive West. Turn left to both the lighthouse and museum.

GEORGIAN HOTEL

Santa Monica, California — — — — — — — — — — —

As with most old buildings, the Georgian Hotel has a long and interesting history. The staff at the hotel is frequently reminded of that history by the spirits who inhabit the building.

The Georgian opened in 1933 as the Lady Windemere and immediately attracted patrons from Hollywood. They came for the secluded environment, the cool ocean breezes, the many amenities offered by the hotel and the beauty of its art deco style. The "Lady" began business at the tail end of the prohibition era and it is believed that the Speakeasy Restaurant, in the lower level of the hotel, was in reality a place where patrons could illegally indulge themselves with alcohol for a short time. These days it seems the restaurant indulges at least one spirit.

In an attempt to prove this, an investigator, using a simple compass, said that readings ranged from north, to west to northwest, indicating some kind of magnetic pull. Since many of the employees reported hearing voices, a tape recorder was set up in the storage room just beside the restaurant. On playing back the tape, no voices from beyond were heard. However, something strange did happen on the tape. Above the door where it was recording, a room air conditioner had been running the entire time, and its hum could be clearly detected in the background—except for about one minute of total silence!

While neither of these tests indicates the presence of a ghost, when combined with the stories from the people who work there, they tend to confirm that something out of the ordinary is happening. Witnesses to these activities abound. Quite a few employees indicated that most of them take place early in the morning. Two waiters reported that on one occasion they were working in the restaurant and heard the sound of high-heeled shoes walking across a wooden floor. When they turned to the front of the restaurant where the sound came from, no one was there. It was then that they remembered that the floor was carpeted. No one else was working with them, leaving them both to wonder if that was a sound from the past.

An electronic beam at the hotel entrance to the restaurant rings a bell, alerting the wait staff to the entrance of a customer. Several employees report hearing the bell, indicating that someone or something had stepped in the path of the beam, yet no one else was around or had entered the restaurant.

Domingo, a cook in the restaurant, has had several experiences with the hotel's spirit. While in the restaurant, he heard someone enter the kitchen. Knowing he was supposed to be working alone, he followed and saw that no one was there. He checked the back door and found no one. Upon hearing glasses rattling, he checked the kitchen again. It was empty.

Another day he heard a man's voice bid him good morning. He replied and looked up. Again he found himself alone. Unable to accept that he'd been greeted by a ghost, he went into the kitchen hoping to find a real person there. What he found instead was that the dishwasher had been turned on. No one else was to be found. The dishwasher requires a few adjustments to be turned on and could not have done so by itself.

Many of the staff have heard unintelligible voices, the sound of silverware rattling, felt a presence following them, and even breathing on their necks, as if someone were standing directly behind them.

During the 1970s and into the eighties, the hotel became a retirement hotel and some people believe there is at least one

The Georgian Hotel's Speakeasy Restaurant

spirit left behind from that time. We were unable to see any evidence confirming those suspicions, but that does not mean those people are wrong. The Speakeasy Restaurant does seem to have some spiritual activity. If you go there, you may find yourself sharing a table with an unidentified spirit from the old speakeasy days. Could it be a Hollywood starlet or Bugsy Siegel? You'll have to decide for yourself.

Address:	**Georgian Hotel** 1415 Ocean Ave. Santa Monica, CA 90401
Phone:	(310) 395-6333 (800) 678-8946

Directions: Take the Pacific Coast Highway to Ocean Avenue. The Georgian is between Santa Monica Boulevard and Broadway.

About the Authors

Ellen Robson and Dianne Halicki live two separate lives in Tempe, Arizona, and Taylor, Michigan, with Route 66 stretched out between them. They first met at a writers' conference on Route 66 where they spent an evening in a cemetery, listening to ghost stories. This first meeting launched a long friendship and a love of storytelling, ghosthunting, and of course, Route 66.

Notes

This work is composed predominately from interviews with the people who live or work in, or have visited, the haunted sites. In some cases further research material was required and is as follows:

Illinois: The account of John Dillinger's death is from the *Chicago Tribune,* July 23, 1934.

There are many accounts of Bachelors' Grove Cemetery. In addition to personal interviews, our information is from Troy Taylor's article "Bachelors' Grove, the Most Haunted Cemetery in Chicago"; *Ghosts of the Prairie* Magazine, Issue 1.

Accounts of former employees' experiences in the Lincoln House appeared in the *State Journal Register,* October 30, 1976.

Missouri: The account of the employee who walked into the deserted *Goldenrod* Showboat is from Jim Longo's *Ghosts Along the Mississippi;* St Anne's Press, St. Louis: 1993.

Kansas: The quote on the description of Quantrill's raids is from William Connelley's *Quantrill and the Border Wars,* p. 377. Torch Press, Cedar Rapids, IA: 1910.

Oklahoma: The story of the ghostly voice at Arapaho Cemetery comes from the article, "Robina Has Not Been Saved," by Martin A. DeHarte. *Fate* Magazine, February, 1982.

ACKNOWLEDGMENTS

We wish to express our thanks to our families, friends, and contributors who gave so much support to our efforts to produce this book. Without the map that Ellen's brother Rich drew for us, we never would have found the haunted sites in the Route 66 city of Springfield, IL. Although it is Ellen's hometown, she soon discovered she had a hard time finding her way around.

Ellen's older brother Charles was kind enough to take a day off work to help us navigate downtown Chicago. We'd still be circling if one of us had been behind the wheel of the car. Five months later when we found ourselves in need of photos, he once again came to our rescue.

Thanks to Ellen's husband John, who didn't complain when she was out on Route 66 ghosthunting with Dianne. And a warm thanks to her children, Eric and Cathi, for their support and encouragement for their Mom's writing career, and most of all, for their love.

A special thanks to all the wonderful people on Route 66 who were willing to share their stories. They invited us into their homes, kept their businesses open late, and gave us tours, from attics to basements. Meeting them was the best part of writing this book!

The authors invite you to share any other ghost stories that you may have heard that occur on or close to Route 66. Please mail them to:

Ellen Robson and Dianne Halicki
Golden West Publishers
4113 N. Longview
Phoenix, AZ 85014

BIBLIOGRAPHY

American Guide Series. Writers' Program of California, 1939.

Campbell, Douglas. *Romancing the Southland.* Hollywood, CA: Romancing the West Publishing, 1994.

Clark, Marian. *The Route 66 Cookbook.* Tulsa: Council Oaks Books, 1993.

Farris, David A. *Mysterious Oklahoma.* Edmond, OK: Little Bruce, 1995.

Gardiner, Colin B. *Ghostwatch.* Slough, Berkshire, England: Foulsham, 1989.

Hauck, Dennis William. *Haunted Places – The National Directory.* New York: Penguin, 1994.

Kaczmarek, Dale. Ghost Trackers Newsletter. June 1997.

Longo, Jim. *Haunted Odyssey.* St. Louis: St. Anne's Press, 1986.

———. *Ghost Along the Mississippi.* St. Louis: St. Anne's Press, 1993.

Looney, Ralph. *Haunted Highways: The Ghosts Towns of New Mexico.* Norwalk, CT: Hastings House, 1968.

Myers, Arthur. *The Ghostly Gazetteer.* Avenel, NJ: Random House, 1995.

Roberts, George, and Jan Roberts. *Discover Historic California.* Baldwin Park, CA: Gem Guides, 1994.

Taylor, Troy. *Haunted Springfield.* Forsyth, IL: Whitechapel Productions, 1997.

Index

ORDER BLANK

GOLDEN WEST PUBLISHERS

☼ 4113 N. Longview Ave. • Phoenix, AZ 85014

www.goldenwestpublishers.com • **1-800-658-5830** • FAX 602-279-6901

Qty	Title	Price	Amount
	Arizona Cook Book	6.95	
	Arizona Territory Cook Book	6.95	
	Arizona Trivia	8.95	
	Best Barbecue Recipes	6.95	
	Billy the Kid Cook Book	7.95	
	Chili-Lovers' Cook Book	6.95	
	Grand Canyon Cook Book	6.95	
	Haunted Arizona: Ghosts of the Grand Canyon State	12.95	
	Haunted Highway: The Spirits of Route 66	12.95	
	Kokopelli's Cook Book	9.95	
	New Mexico Cook Book	6.95	
	Oklahoma Cook Book	6.95	
	Quick-n-Easy Mexican Recipes	6.95	
	Real New Mexico Chile	6.95	
	Salsa Lovers Cook Book	6.95	
	Take This Chile & Stuff It!	6.95	
	Tequila Cook Book	7.95	
	Texas Cook Book	6.95	
	Tortilla Lovers Cook Book	6.95	
	Western Breakfasts	7.95	

Shipping & Handling Add: United States $3.00
Canada & Mexico $5.00—All others $12.00

☐ My Check or Money Order Enclosed

☐ MasterCard ☐ VISA ($20 credit card minimum)

Total $ _____

(Payable in U.S. funds)

Acct. No. _____ Exp. Date _____

Signature _____

Name _____ Phone _____

Address _____

City/State/Zip _____

Call for a FREE catalog of all of our titles

1/03   This order blank may be photocopied   Haunted Highway